MONETIZE YOUR BLOG
STEP BY STEP

Learn How To Make Money Blogging. Leverage Digital Marketing Best
Practices And Create Digital Products To Profit From Your Blog

JACOB GREEN

COPYRIGHT

Table of contents

Introduction

The answer to this question is indeed simple but only if you understand its meaning. Blog stands for web log which is a type of internet service. People who write blogs are known as bloggers. It provides an opportunity to the bloggers to post content online which are usually theme based. It can be considered to be a diary where you can write your views. They are reverse in chronological order. They were initially started in the 1990s and they gained immense popularity in 2004. It is a type of social networking site which the bloggers can use for their personal or professional purpose. Some publishers use their blogs to advertise and publish their books. The books that are published using blogs are known as "Blooks".

Different Types Of Blogs Are Given Below:

Blogs are mainly of two types. The first type of blogs are personal blogs where the bloggers write some of their life's important events. The second type of blogs are the corporation or organizational blogs. The organizational blogs are mostly used for advertising purposes. The organizational bloggers are generally businessmen, servicemen, and so on. They want to advertise their products and keep their viewers updated on different business events taking place. They can also use their blogs to advertise customer or sales comments. This is to help people read about a particular product before they purchase it.

The personal blogs are mostly used to update the bloggers' family members, friends and relatives about the latest events going on in their lives. Some people also use personal blogs to vent their frustration by expressing their feelings and thoughts.

Rules of Conduct

- ✓ You will be responsible for all the activities done on your blog. This includes the comments your viewers leave and the comments left by you.

- ✓ Make it clear to all your visitors that no abuse will be tolerated.

- ✓ You should immediately clear off all offensive and annoying comments.

- ✓ If you find a person giving negative or offensive comments then caution them immediately.

- ✓ If you want to say some personal things to someone, don't use blogs to do so.

Now, have you got the answer to what is blogging? Those who know how to make full use of blogging find it really interesting. Moreover, blogs can be financially beneficial for your business and organization. On the other hand, you will receive negative comments if you show your anger or frustration on your blog. Keeping your blog clean and avoiding negative comments will help you build a good reputation. It will also create a positive impression on those people who read your blog.

What is the purpose of a blog?

There are many reasons for starting a personal blog and only a handful of strong ones for business blogging. Blogging for business, projects, or anything else that might bring you money has a very straightforward purpose – to rank your website higher in Google SERPs, a.k.a. increase your visibility.

As a business, you rely on consumers to keep buying your products and services. As a new business, you rely on blogging to help you get to these consumers and grab their attention. Without blogging, your website would remain invisible, whereas running a blog makes you searchable and competitive.

So, the main purpose of a blog is to connect you to the relevant audience. Another one is to boost your traffic and send quality leads to your website.

The more frequent and better your blog posts are, the higher the chances for your website to get discovered and visited by your target audience. Which means, a blog is an effective lead generation tool. Add a great call to action (CTA), and it will convert your website traffic into high-quality leads. But a blog also allows you to showcase your authority and build a brand.

When you use your niche knowledge for creating informative and engaging posts, it builds trust with your audience. Great blogging makes your business look more credible, which is especially important if your brand is still young and fairly unknown. It ensures presence and authority at the same time.

Blog structure

The appearance of blogs changed over time, and nowadays blogs include different items. But, most blogs include some standard features and structure. Here are some common features that a typical blog will include:

- ✔ Header with the menu or navigation bar

- ✔ Main content area with highlighted or latest blog posts

- ✔ Sidebar with social profiles, favorite content, or call-to-action

- ✔ Footer with relevant links like a disclaimer, privacy policy, contact page, etc.

Blogs and websites

A majority of people still wonder whether there is any difference between a blog and a website. What is a blog and what is a website? It's even more challenging to differentiate between the two today. Many companies are integrating blogs into their sites to perform the same function.

What differentiates blogs from websites?

Blogs need frequent updates. Good examples include a food blog sharing meal recipes or a company writing about their industry news.

Blogs promote perfect reader engagement. Readers get a chance to comment and voice their different concerns to the viewer. Static websites, on the other hand, consists of the content presented on static pages. Static website owners rarely update their pages. Blog owners update their site with new blog posts on a regular basis.

Key elements that identify a blog post from a static page include a publishing date, author reference, categories, and tags within a byline. While not all blog posts have all those byline elements, static website pages do not have any of these items. From a visitor perspective, the content on a static site will not change from one visit to the next. The content on a blog, yet, has the potential to offer something new each day, week, or month. Depending on the blog owner's publishing schedule.

In the early 2000s, blogging emerged in all different phases when several political blogs were born. Also, blogs with how-to manuals began to appear. Established institutions began to note the difference between journalism and blogging. The number of bloggers in the United States is set to reach 31.7 million users in 2020.

Definition of blogging

Blogging is the set of many skills that one needs to run and control a blog. Equipping web page with tools to make the process of writing, posting, linking, and sharing content easier on the internet.

Why is blogging so popular?

It's important to mention that blogging grows with each passing day! Hence, to answer the question 'what is blogging' we need to look at the factors behind its rise.

In the early stages, blogs became mainstream, as news services began using them as tools for outreach and opinion forming. It became a new source of information.

Businesses saw a good way to improve the customer's level of satisfaction. Through blogging, companies keep clients and customers up to date. The more people visit your blog, the more exposure and trust your brand gets.

Personal and niche bloggers, saw the potential to reach

more people interested in specific topics. Through a blog, visitors can comment and interact with you or your brand which helps you create a network of loyal followers.

Did you know you could earn money through blogging? Once your blog gets enough attention and fans, you can look into ways of monetizing your blog. Through the blog, you can offer your services and sell products.

<u>Who is a blogger?</u>

In recent times, bloggers have become famous for various reasons. An alternative career or job to many, more people are choosing to join the ranks. So who are bloggers? These are individuals who love sharing parts of their lives with you. They post various topics from arts, home designs, carpentry, and finance articles. Bloggers are mobile and don't need to be in one place. They live on the internet!

Why are many people blogging today?

Would you want to have a blog of your own? Yes! Most people today are creating a blog for various reasons. Every human being has its story to tell. Hence, through the internet, bloggers can communicate to a larger group of people.

Why is blogging so popular? Blogs allow you to talk about any topics and express your opinion. You'll find some bloggers writing on every activity that took place during the day. These may range from small issues such as waking up, to major issues like human rights and climate changes! Remember that as a blogger running your own blog, you need to rely on the topics that you love and strive to become one of the best blogs on the web.

Are bloggers getting paid?

Bloggers do earn money, but this is not a get-rich-quick kind of profession. Before you can start monetizing your blog, you need to build both your Google SERPs ranking and your niche influence. And that takes plenty of time and quality content. Money-making opportunities won't present themselves until you've gained some credibility in the field. So, get down to business.

Here's how you can make good money as a top-ranked niche blogger:

- ✓ Selling ad space on your blog privately or via Google AdSense.

- ✓ Becoming an affiliate partner privately or through ad networks.

- ✓ Selling your own digital products such as eBooks and tutorials.

- ✓ Selling memberships for access to exclusive content or advice.

- ✓ Using your blog as a content marketing tool for your business.

If you're starting a blog as a way to market and boost your existing business, you probably won't be selling ad space or memberships. But you can create and start offering exclusive digital products such as eBooks, guides, or online courses as a lead capturing tool in exchange for visitors' email addresses. That way, you'll nudge them one step further down your sales funnel.

Do you want to start a blog?

Creating your own personal blog takes a few steps. First, you need to decide on a name for your blog also called a domain name, and choose the best blogging platform. We recommend going with the self-hosted platform. There are few choices when it comes to self-hosted platforms but the most popular is WordPress.org.

Then you need to choose a web hosting service and for new bloggers, we strongly recommend Bluehost, a company that powers over 2 million websites worldwide. You will get a Free domain name when you sign up with them and if you don't like their services, they offer a 30-day money-back guarantee.

How to Decide What to Write About on Your Blog

Most people start blogging to express themselves, whether through random thoughts, or as a way of keeping daily records of their lives or travels, by writing poetry or short stories or by putting up their photographs.

In most cases what begins as a mish mash of things slowly but surely begins to take a shape. After making several posts, the blog begins to take on a distinct personality. It becomes a blog on a certain topic, subject, issue, reason, genre or even of a certain kind of tone (say humorous or sarcastic).

For most people it gets very difficult to decide beforehand what they are exactly going to blog on. What their blog's topic or even tone and style will be. All of this develops as the blog develops.

This book will give all the regular netizens and blogging newbies simple guidelines on how to decide what to blog on. It will act like a simple guide on how to choose a blogging topic, subject, genre or tone.

By sheer common sense, the simplest way to decide on what your blog topic should be is through elimination. Let us begin by eliminating one of two basic kinds of blogs - the personal blog and the non-personal blog.

Very broadly, blogs can either be personal or non-personal. Personal blogs are about your own thoughts, views, artistic self-expression through art, music, poetry, videos or anything at all of a personal nature.

Non-personal blogs are based on anything that is not of a personal nature. It could be on other people's views, thoughts, lives, art, music, interests etc. and may or may not have your own added views in them.

Let us take examples to explain this better. Suppose you start a blog in which you write about your experiences while traveling across the world, it becomes a blog about you, and what happened to you. It becomes a personal blog.

On the other hand if you have a blog that is centred on the best movies being released in Hollywood, it become a non-personal blog. Even if you express your views on these movies, they are non-personal, because your main subject is not you, or anything created or written basis your own experiences or self-expression.

Well, let us now assume that you have eliminated non-personal blogs. Now you are left with the arena of personal blogs. Personal blogs can be broadly and very rudimentarily divided into three types - your experiences, any form of self-expression or your personal views.

If you now decide to eliminate self-expression and personal views, you are left with experiences. Blogs on personal experiences can of many kinds, but let us for the sake of simplicity take these: Travel experiences, Daily experiences, Professional experiences, Recreational experiences, Spiritual Experiences, Relationship experiences.

Suppose you zoom in to recreational experiences, then you have a plethora of choices - eating experiences, partying experiences, sports experiences, cinematic experiences, theatre experiences and others.

Now, suppose that you decide to eliminate all except eating experiences. You have finally come down to a very specific topic to blog on. You will blog on all the gastronomic experiences you have in the course of your life. Be it eating in an obscure restaurant in your home town, or having the local food of Hawaii or the special dinner your wife cooked. You will be writing on your experiences with food, and that becomes the topic of your blog.

Quite simple, but there is the hurdle of a large number of choices. However this hurdle becomes a blessing, because you will never be able to identify all the choices, and will maybe identify only a few of the. The good thing about that is that is that if you could not think of certain choices, it is because you actually aren't even interested in them. Thus they get automatically eliminated.

Similarly if you had eliminated personal and chosen non-personal, you would go about in a similar manner to eliminate the choices and reach the right one. As a rudimentary example, we could say that there are choices like celebrity, technology, finance, books, nature etc. Using the same method as we did for the personal blogs, and with your imagination and common sense, you will be able to quickly find out exactly what you want to blog on.

If you have been online for any amount of time you will notice that there are literally thousands upon thousands of blogs on the internet. It shouldn't surprise us any, as the majority of people on the internet are content hungry. Google in fact rewards websites that post new updated content frequently. Content is King. How many times have you heard that statement before? There is a reason you've heard it so many times.

The internet revolves around content. If you have an online business you should be posting new content on a regular basis. The best way to do this, and by far the easiest, is to have a blog. Post articles, product reviews, product announcements, tips on a particular subject or niche. The possibilities are virtually endless when it comes to the type of content you can post on your blog.

Blogger and Wordpress are the most popular blogging software. Blogger is very easy to use and setup. Your blog can be hosted on the Blogger domain, or on your own domain. Wordpress is the same as far as the hosting goes; however, the features available are a lot more complex. Wordpress has many powerful features that are at your disposal, and it can be a little hard to figure everything out. There are many tutorials and videos on how to use Wordpress and all the add-ons that it has.

Once you have your blog setup, it's time to start posting. You want to provide relevant information about whatever topic you want to write about. Provide information that will help your readers. Post as often as possible and your readers will stay loyal to you. Once you have a following, you can monetize on the traffic your blog is bringing in. There are many ways to do this, and I will point out a couple of them.

One way you can be making money blogging is by putting Google AdSense ads on your blog. Advertisers pay a fee, a cost per click, to have their ads placed on other people's websites. When a visitor comes to your blog and clicks on one of the ads, you get paid a percentage of the cost. This is a great way to earn some extra income with your blog.

Another way you can be making money blogging is by signing up for an affiliate program and advertising it on your blog. The program should relate to the content of your blog. If someone signs up for the program through you, you get paid a commission. Depending on the program, you can even get paid every month for each member you refer. You can also sell individual products as an affiliate. Great places to find products are at either Clickbank or Commission Junction.

These are just a couple out of many other ways that you can be making money blogging. Use your imagination and get creative. Blogging can be fun, but it is also hard work posting new content every day. It will take a lot of time and effort, but if you are serious it can be done. Any online business should provide a blog for their readers because it is a good way to help their website rank in search engines. Hopefully you will have a better understanding of what blogging is and how you can make money with it after going through all the chapters encompassed in this book.

Chapter One
Step By Step Process To Make Money From Blogging

Most of us are feeling the effects of the economic downturn that seems to be going around the world. In an effort to make additional money, people are willing to do almost anything. However, one legitimate, and easy way for you to earn some additional income, however, is by having a website on the Internet. Even if you are not technically minded, it is possible for you to get started if you just follow some simple steps. Although there are a number of different ways for you to do this, we are going to go through some steps of how to make money from blogging. You would probably be surprised with how easy it is.

First of all, you do not even need to invest any money in order to get started. However, I always suggest that somebody purchase a domain name and get some inexpensive hosting in order to give themselves a more professional look. There are some free blogging platforms, however, such as Blogger.com which will give you the ability to put advertising on a free blog. You can get started with these rather easily, simply by following the step-by-step setup process. Add the advertising to your account and start blogging on a daily basis. Soon you will have enough money in order to get started with a more professional setup.

One of the big secrets of how to make money from blogging

is to focus on one subject. It doesn't necessarily matter what that subject is, but it is always easier if you start out talking about something that you are personally interested in. Make sure that you stay focused on that one subject, especially considering the fact that many of your readers are going to return to find out what else you have to say.

Another thing that you should make sure that you are doing is being persistent in posting to the blog. It isn't really necessary for you to post every day although that is not a bad practice to get into. How to make money from blogging has more to do with you setting up a schedule and following it faithfully. Before you know it, people will be visiting on a regular basis, commenting on your blog posts and even inviting other people to visit. That is when you will realize your goal of making money on the Internet.

You want to make money, right? Of course you do. Everyone wants – and needs -to make money. So you started a blog since you've heard it's an easy way to make cash, but you're not quite sure how to actually make money doing it. Or maybe you already have a blog and you're exploring ways to monetize it.

No matter which group you're in, making money with a blog – whether it's a hobby blog or a business blog –is possible. It's not a get rich quick ordeal, but if you do it right, you could make enough to support your family and more. Let's dive in and see how you can make a profit with your blog. When you think of how to make money blogging, advertising is often the first thing that comes to mind.

Yes, it is possible to make money with ads on WordPress, but there are also other ways you can monetize your blog content. Here are a few methods that work:

1. Make Money With Affiliate Marketing

Affiliate marketing is when you recommend a product or service to your audience using special tracking links, and then get a referral commission for every time someone buys after clicking your link.

A real-life example of affiliate marketing would be when you help a friend open a bank account at your bank branch. Usually, they give you a gift card or a bonus of some sort.

Similar to that many products and services online have affiliate programs that you can join. There are affiliate programs available for every industry (niche).

If you're interested in getting started with affiliate marketing, you can start by thinking about the products you already use that your readers may be interested in as well. Then you can see if they have an affiliate program that you can sign up for.

You can find a huge list of products to promote from:

- ✓ Amazon
- ✓ Commission Junction
- ✓ ShareASale

Once you have selected the products to promote, then you can use a WordPress plugin like PrettyLinks to manage your affiliate links. It allows you to quickly insert links into posts, create branded links, auto-replace keywords into links, and even see how each link is performing on your site.

Affiliate marketing is the easiest way to make money

because you can promote a wide-variety of products. Just about every popular store like Walmart, BestBuy, Amazon, and others have an affiliate program.

To learn more, see our beginner's guide to affiliate marketing and also check out these affiliate marketing tools and plugins which will help you increase your earnings.

2. Display Google AdSense on WordPress

Google Adsense is an easy way to make money from your blog. All you need to do is add a script from Google to your website and start displaying ads. You will get paid every time a user clicks on the ad. These are called CPC ads.

What is CPC? CPC stands for "cost per click." By displaying CPC ads with Google Adsense, you receive a set fee every time a visitor clicks on an ad.

The cost per click is set by the advertiser. (This is in contrast to CPM ads, where you're paid for ad views instead of clicks. CPM means "cost per thousand impressions," where M is the roman numeral for 1,000.) Google Adsense is a good way to start earning money online when you are first starting out.

3. Use a WordPress Advertising Plugin to Sell Ads Directly

Google AdSense is easy to set up, but the amount of money you can earn is limited. Each ad click earning will vary. Directly selling banner ad space on your website can be more lucrative. Instead of having to rely on an intermediary who takes a cut of the money, you negotiate the price and terms on your own.

Above we mentioned the difference between CPC and CPM

ads, where you are paid per click or per thousand views. While you could use one of those models for selling banner ads, most bloggers charge a flat rate instead. Charging a flat rate is easier than keeping track of views or clicks.

Still, directly selling ads takes more work to manage than using Google AdSense. Instead of just adding a bit of code to your website, you'll have to negotiate the pricing, come up with an agreement and terms, and take care of administrative work like invoicing.

However, using a WordPress ad management plugin can make the process easier. We recommend using AdSanity, it allows you to manage Google AdSense as well as your own ads.

4. Sell Sponsored Blog Posts

Some bloggers aren't interested in displaying ads to their audience and wonder how to monetize a blog without ads.

With ad networks, you lose some control over the content displayed on your site. Some readers will get annoyed or offended by ads, and more and more people are using ad blockers which affects your earning potential.

An alternative way to monetize a blog is through sponsorships.

A sponsorship works just like it does in sports, TV shows, or other industries. Basically, a company pays you to represent their product, talk about it, and promote it to your readers.

To get started, it's a good idea to put together a one-page media kit that details your traffic stats, social media following, audience demographics, and any other data that will make your site more appealing to advertisers. Then, you can approach companies to negotiate a sponsorship deal. When publishing sponsored posts, it's crucial to know about the laws in your area about disclosure.

For example, in the United States, a blogger who publishes a sponsored post must comply with the FTC's Endorsement Guides. This includes disclosing whenever a post is sponsored. You can do that by adding a sponsored post prefix to your post title in WordPress.

5. Get Paid to Write Reviews

Similar to sponsored posts, you can also make money by writing paid reviews on your site.

This is a slightly different monetization method than a review site with affiliate links, as mentioned above. Instead, you get to try out products related to your niche for free, and even get paid for writing a review.

The process for doing this can be similar to getting sponsored posts. You'll want to review products that are relevant to your niche, that your audience would be interested in. You can approach companies on your own to ask about doing paid reviews. There are also websites like PayPerPost that can help to connect you with businesses who may be interested.

6. Earn Money Online by Flipping Websites

If you know how to build a WordPress website, then you're way ahead of most people. Sometimes entrepreneurs like to buy already established websites that they can use for their own businesses. If you can build a WordPress blog and start getting traffic to it, then you can sell it and make money for your efforts.

This requires knowing the type of websites in demand, and how to price and sell them. There are websites like Flippa that serve as auction sites and brokers for selling websites.

7. Get Public Speaking Gigs as an Influencer

If you are promoting your own brand along with your blog, then over time you will get a decent following establishing you as an influencer in your space. You can utilize this recognition to get some public speaking jobs. Many bloggers make a lot of money by speaking at conferences.

Speaking at events whether you are paid or not helps you promote your blog and your personal brand. If you are good at networking and public speaking, then you would be able to find lots of new opportunities.

Here are some general tips you need to keep in mind if you want to make money as a paid public speaker:

- ✓ Be an expert in your field. If you don't have enough knowledge/skills at the moment, then start learning right away.

- ✓ Be consistent – You need to continuously promote your expertise on the topic through your blogging and social media activities.

- ✓ Let people know that you are available. You can announce on social media or privately reach out to event organizers.

- ✓ You may not find paid public speaking gigs right away. Many successful speakers start their public speaking career from smaller, more casual, and free community events and meetups.

✓ Create a Paid Membership Website

✓ make money online with paid membership sites

If you're not interested in selling ads or sponsored posts, there are plenty of other ways you can earn money online from your blog. A popular method is by having your audience pay to access certain content or areas of your site. Here are a couple of ways to do that.

8. Create Restricted Members Only Content

Your most loyal readers are huge fans and may be willing to pay to read more of your work. You can create a members-only area for them to share more in-depth blog posts, downloads, videos, audio content, and more.

Membership sites can be a big time investment since you must continually create premium content for your paying members. But they can be very lucrative because they are recurring revenue (subscriptions). You can easily create a membership site using a WordPress membership plugin. We recommend using MemberPress, it is the most beginner friendly and robust membership plugin for WordPress.

9. Create a Private Forum

Another option for creating a paid membership site is to create private forums that users must pay to get access to. Forums are a great way for your audience to get one-on-one advice from you. Other members of the community can also interact and help each other out.

While moderating a forum can be a lot of work, a paid forum is a great way to earn recurring revenue from your WordPress site. To get started, you'll need to set up a forum on your site.

10. Create a questions and answers community

Question and answers communities like Stack Exchange and Quora are huge. They help you build an online community that is driven, motivated, and highly engaged.

Just like forums, you will have to spend some time building a sizable community. After that, you will be able to monetize user-generated content on your website using advertisements, affiliate ads, and other methods.

Popular question and answer websites are able to get direct advertisement and sponsorship deals from advertisers in their industry. This helps them negotiate a much higher rate and extra perks.

Another option for making money online with WordPress is to create a directory or listing website. You can then charge visitors to advertise their listings on your site.

Here are a few different directory ideas to get you started:

11. Create a Paid Business Directory

Web directories may make you think of the early days of the web before bots started indexing everything automatically, but they're not completely obsolete. Generic web directories are no longer necessary, but local or niche directories can be extremely useful.

Directories might gather reviews of local businesses, share the best podcasts on a given topic, or list the best products in a certain niche.

You can easily create a web directory in WordPress

following the information in this book. There are also plenty of directory plugins for WordPress you can choose from, many of which allow you to accept payments with submissions.

12. Create a WordPress Job Board With Paid Submissions

Another option is to create a paid job board. Companies who want to advertise an open position to your audience can pay you to submit a listing. It's easier to create a successful job board if you narrow down to a specific niche. That way you can become the go-to site for anyone looking for a job in that industry, with minimal competition.

This works great for established blogs in a narrow niche. For example, ProBlogger is now famous for their job board for professional bloggers.

13. Create a WordPress Event Calendar With Paid Submissions

Instead of a job board, you could create an event calendar where you charge people to advertise their events. This also works well if you already have an established audience, because businesses will be willing to pay to reach your audience.

A paid event calendar is a good monetization method for local or industry-specific websites. You might choose to advertise events in your local city, conferences in a certain industry, or even webinars or live streaming events.

If you're looking for a more low-maintenance way to make money online blogging with WordPress, then selling your own digital products may be a good choice. While you do have to invest the time to create the product up front, after it's created your work is very minimal.

Here are a few digital products you can create and sell on your website.

14. Sell Ebooks on WordPress

Ebooks are an obvious choice for creating digital products. They are relatively simple to write and produce. If you've been blogging for a while, then you can collect some of your old blog posts and turn them into chapters of a book.

Once your book is written, you can design a cover using a tool like Canva and create a PDF of your ebook. Selling digital products on WordPress is easy with a plugin.

For digital downloads, we recommend Easy Digital Downloads. It's relatively easy to use and includes all the features you need to create your online store.

15. Sell Online Courses

Selling an online course is another great way to make money online. Courses usually sell for a much higher price point than ebooks. You can charge a premium for your expertise.

You'll need to create the lessons for your course, plus any supporting materials that you want to include such as downloads, slides, checklists, templates, etc.

You will also need to decide whether you want to offer personalized support for your course. Some sites offer two tiers of each course: a basic version without support, and a premium version with email support. Once your course is ready, you can use a learning management system (LMS) plugin to deliver the course to your audience.

16. Host a Paid Webinar

Webinars are a great way to build your audience, share your experience, and grow your business. But did you know they're also a smart way to make money online? Webinars are similar to online courses, but a webinar is live and often includes a question and answer section.

WordPress makes it easy to host a paid webinar. Whether you're using your site to actually host the webinar, or just to advertise your webinar and register participants, it's crucial for your webinar success. If you're looking for easy ways to make money online, selling services is the fastest way to get started. There's no up front investment of creating a product or investing in inventory. Instead, you can just create a "hire me" page on your website and start looking for your first client.

Here are a few ideas to get you started.

17. Offer Freelance Services

As a blogger, you're already an expert on your niche. You can start earning an income by offering your skills and expertise as a freelancer. Freelancing is a popular way to make money online because it doesn't necessarily require any upfront investment of time or money. You can just start offering your services to your current audience.

Once you start freelancing, you'll need a way to invoice and collect payments from your clients. We recommend using FreshBooks, but there are also other invoicing plugins for WordPress.

If you're interested in freelancing to make some serious money online, then see our list of the top tools for WordPress freelancers, designers, and developers for help getting started.

18.Start Your Own Consulting Business

Consulting is another way to make money online from your blog and share your expertise.

Instead of offering your services, a consultant offers advice and strategy so that their clients can become more effective. As with freelancing, there is no startup investment. You can start offering consulting services on your existing blog. All you need is to create a page with a form so users can request more information. To easily create a professional, mobile-friendly form, I recommend WPForms.

19.Become a Coach

If "consultant" doesn't feel like the right title for you, you can consider becoming a coach instead.

A life coach offers advice, guidance, and accountability for setting goals and improving one's life. There are also other kinds of coaches, such as blog coaches, writing coaches, and more. Whatever your area of expertise is, you can provide one-on-one help to your audience with coaching sessions.

To save time and make things convenient for your clients, you can set up a booking form so readers can schedule coaching sessions right from your WordPress blog.

Sell Physical Products Online Using WordPress

While selling digital products or services can be an easy way to start making money online, there's nothing quite like selling real, physical products. Here are a few ways you can get started selling products with WordPress.

20. Start an Ecommerce Business With WooCommerce

Have an idea for your own product? Why not start your own online store?

WordPress makes it easy to create a shop or even add a shop to your existing blog using the free WooCommerce plugin. Starting an online store can be a lot of work, since you need to create or buy the products and then ship them out yourself. But selling physical products can be a rewarding experience, and sometimes a physical product is exactly what your audience wants. You can also use Shopify or BigCommerce as WooCommerce alternatives.

21. Create an Online T-shirt Store With WordPress

Creating your own t-shirt shop is easy with WordPress. Almost everyone wears t-shirts, so opening up a t-shirt shop is a great way to monetize any kind of blog. Designing t-shirts allows you to be creative and offer something unique to your audience.

It's easy because there are services out there that allow you to upload your own designs, and they print / ship it for you. You get a profit share. You can easily create your own t-shirt shop on your WordPress site using WP-Spreadplugin by Spreadshirt.

Open your own online tshirt store to make money. If you want a faster solution, then you can use a Shopify store which connects with dozens of t-shirt printing companies.

22. Create a WooCommerce Dropshipping Store

Dropshipping is another way you can create an ecommerce store on your WordPress website without having to handle inventory or ship items yourself.

With dropshipping, you create the store, manage the website, and customer service. But a dropshipping service will take your orders and ship them out to your customers. They're an invisible third party that your customers don't even know about.

You can use the WooCommerce plugin to create a dropshipping store. There's also a WooCommerce Dropshipping addon plugin that allows you to automate the process.

23. Create an Amazon Affiliate WordPress Shop

One downside of dropshipping is that you have to find a good supplier, which can be a challenge, and sometimes you have to place a large order up front. This can make it difficult to get started without investing a lot of money. If you want an easier way to set up an ecommerce site without having to ship products yourself, then you may want to try an Amazon Affiliate shop.

As with many of the items on this list, this works best if you specialize in a niche. If you offer everything, it's impossible to compete with a big shop like Amazon. But in a small niche, you can differentiate yourself and really stand out.

For complete instructions, see our tutorial on how to create an Amazon affiliate store using WordPress.

Offering Platform as a Service

WordPress comes with some incredibly powerful plugins that are actually full-fledged platforms in their own right. You can add such a platform to your blog or e-commerce store and offer it as a paid service. You get a cut from each sell, which allows you to earn passive income from user activity on your website.

24. Create an Online Marketplace Website

An online marketplace is like an eCommerce store where users cannot just buy but also sell their own products. Normally, WooCommerce assumes that you run a single vendor website.

You will need a plugin like WC Vendors to turn WooCommerce into a multi-vendor capable platform. After that, vendors will be able to register on your site and start selling. You can make money by charging commission on each sell, or you can allow vendors to buy membership packages for their listings.

25. Make an Auctions Website

An auctions website allows users to bid on products to purchase them. This allows the sellers to maximize their profits and customers to find unique deals. Ebay is probably the best example of an online auctions marketplace.

You can run auctions on your WordPress website and even allow third-party vendors to list their products as well. You can make money by charging for the listing or by getting a cut on each sell.

To build an auctions marketplace with WordPress, you will need the following add-ons.

- ✓ WooCommerce (for shopping cart and payment features).
- ✓ An auctions add-on
- ✓ A multi-vendor add-on

26. Create a Job Marketplace website

Unlike a regular job listings website, a job marketplace allows you to make money on each job listing. Fiverr and UpWork are probably the best examples of online job marketplace websites.

You can promote your job marketplace as a micro-job platform for people working in the same niche as your blog. To make your platform more competitive you can select a very specific niche. This will help you easily find customers and professionals who are unable to use large platforms because of too much irrelevant competition.

You can charge a small fee for job listings or when a job is completed. More successful completion of jobs will bring you more customers and freelancers in the future.

If you're more technically inclined, then you can become a WordPress developer or designer in order to make money online. This will take more technical skills, but it's not too hard to get started.

27. Develop WordPress Plugins

Plugins are what make WordPress so flexible and powerful. Plugins work like apps, allowing you to extend and modify any feature of your WordPress website. Plugins come in all varieties, from very simple code modifications to complex software applications. If you have a basic grasp of how WordPress works and some simple PHP knowledge, you can create your own WordPress plugin.

As a plugin developer, there are many ways you can distribute your plugins. Anyone can submit a free plugin to the WordPress.org plugin directory, as long as they follow the WordPress plugin guidelines. This is a great way to gain experience and build a reputation for yourself as a WordPress plugin developer.

Once you're ready to start selling premium plugins, you can choose to sell them on a site like MOJO Marketplace, or on your own WordPress site.

If you're using your existing WordPress blog to sell plugins, you'll want to make sure that the plugin you create directly fulfills a need of your audience. You can survey them to see what problems they need to solve on their WordPress site, and then create a plugin that solves that problem. You can then sell the plugin on your site using Easy Digital Downloads.

28. Sell WordPress Themes

If you enjoy web design and development, you could start creating your own WordPress themes to sell. This requires both design and technical skills. You have to know how to create a good-looking design, and also how to code it for WordPress.

Using a WordPress theme framework such as Genesis can give you a head start. Then you'll need to design and code a beautiful child theme.

29. Sell Graphics on Your WordPress Site

If you like design more than coding, another option is to design and sell graphics on your WordPress site. You can create graphics such as stock images or logos and sell them on your site using an ecommerce plugin. You can also join online marketplaces to sell your graphics as well.

30. Accept Donations

Last but not least, one way you can make money from your WordPress blog is simply by asking for donations. You can begin accepting donations in a few different ways. You could add a Paypal donate button or a Stripe donate button to your website. Or for a more professional look and advanced features like email marketing integration, you could use WPForms to create a donation form on your WordPress site. Donations are last on the list because of their limited effectiveness, since you have to rely on the generosity of your readers. It's usually more lucrative to offer them something in return.

We have heard almost every question you can think of. Here are the top questions beginners ask us about making money online by blogging.

31. Which one of these proven ways is right for me?

Depends on what you are passionate about and which method would work best with your blog's topics.

For example, if you run a blog about photography, then affiliate marketing, advertisements, and paid memberships may all work well for your blog.

Focus on offering useful, quality content, that users will find helpful and money will follow. Or as the saying goes, do what you love and the money will follow.

32. How much money can I make from blogging?

It really depends on how much effort you put in and the time you are willing to invest. To be honest, many beginner bloggers lose interest and give up quickly.

You will be making money based on how much traffic you get, the monetization methods you use, and the work you put in. Many successful bloggers make six and even seven figure incomes.

33. How long would it take before I start making some serious money from blogging?

Making money online is not a 'get-rich-quick' scam. Anyone telling you otherwise is probably trying to scam you. If you want to make money by starting a blog, then you will have to work hard and invest a lot of your time into it.

There is no easy way to tell you how soon you would start making money. Some bloggers start making small amounts soon after starting their blogs. Others struggle to get their blogs to take off. However, those who continuously work and stick to a planned strategy are the ones most likely to see encouraging results very early on.

34. How do I get started?

Getting started with your own WordPress blog is easy. However, make sure that you are using the right platform. Basically, there are two types of WordPress available. WordPress.com which is a hosted solution, and

WordPress.org, also known as self-hosted WordPress.

We recommend using WordPress.org because it will allow you to start making money without any limitations.

You will need a domain name and a web hosting account to start blogging with WordPress.org. Normally, a domain costs $14.99 per year and web hosting $7.99 per month usually paid for a full year.

Basically, you will be able to get started for just $2.75 per month. Bluehost is an officially recommended WordPress hosting provider and one of the largest hosting companies in the world.

After purchasing hosting, you will be ready to install WordPress. Follow the instructions in our step by step guide on how to start a blog which will help you get started in less than 30 minutes.

Chapter Two
How To Choose The Right Niche

Marketers have today woken up to the rich potentials of niche marketing that is generally ignored by mainstream marketers. And for promoting a niche product, one should ideally run a blog that belongs to that specific niche. Niche blogs usually contain information on comparatively lesser known products, features, places, or populations in a way that will help marketers' niche marketing efforts. Identifying a niche in itself can sometimes be difficult because of the very limited information available. An extensive search through web sites or books about unheard of places or ideas or goods will have to be done to zero in on a proper niche.

A good blog niche can be selected through trial and error experiments. To start with, you can create blogs on a few 'out of the mainstream' topics and have them placed in directories or other places where there is likely to be a reasonable amount of web traffic. The blogs should ideally be short, just about a couple of paragraphs only, since they are being done on an experimental basis. And the opening sentences of the blog should capture the essence of the blog so that you are able to convey the gist of the subject with just those two sentences. If the readers are interested in the topic, they would read through the whole blog, especially since they will be short and will not take away much of their time.

After a few trial blogs, you will be able to identify the readers' interests. You will be able to make out the topics they are keen on reading and the services they are likely to be more interested in. Once you have identified their needs, you will have to do an equal amount of research to identify the products and services that are likely to be useful to them. This too will take some time, since equipments and services that cater exclusively to isolated segments of populations are not easy to come by. It may take some time to come across such products. However, sometimes you may also be able to tailor some existing products for their use as well.

By identify the market segment and the products that they are likely to need, you have crossed the first two hurdles. The next job is to find out a provider of those goods that you and your niche population need. This is likely to be the least difficult of the jobs since internet abounds with products of all sorts, and merchants eager to promote their goods through different channels. Working together with them will help you to identify the right product for the niche market you are targeting. If you want to be part of an affiliate marketing program and promote products through your blog to the market segment that you have identified, streamline your blog in that direction. You will have to get the necessary affiliate links from the merchant for placement on your blog and web site. By sending customers to the merchant's web site through proper channels, you will be able to become part of a successful affiliate program and earn a good income.

First, let's take a look at John Chow. John is a savvy marketer. Even though he says he just rambles on in his blog posts, he's really quite the intelligent marketer who knows about all of the most popular topics that people are interested in reading. He talks about fast cars, traveling, cooking, family, electronics and his interesting life making a lot of money as a blogger... more than $400,000 per year.

Talking about all of those hot topics in his blog is incredibly smart marketing and the reasons why John Chow has a large following. With a large following comes a large email list, and with a large email list comes a lot of income.

Next, let's take a look at a young kid by the name of Michael Dunlap. Michael earned a six figure income from blogging by the time he was 18 years old. He now makes upwards of $10,000 a day, because he stuck it out for the duration in a popular niche. It only took him a few short years to accomplish making the big bucks.

Michael teaches people about making money as a blogger. He also follows the basic marketing rules that every other successful blogger follows.

Michael makes money teaching people about making money, and that's exactly what you will be doing, even though you will be blogging on your niche... that is, if you want to be successful.

If your popular niche can reach out to people and make a difference in their life, and if you sell blogging products and services from your blog at the same time, you will be successful beyond your imagination.

Is there something you love to do and know that you can help other people with your knowledge? Is your passion (your niche) in an industry where people all over the world will have a huge interest? If it is, you are off to a good start, and you could turn your passion into a nice income in this blogging business. If you want to make a nice living blogging, you will need to learn how to blog about something that you love, but also interests hundreds of thousands of people.

Choosing your niche is where you will need to be careful. You might feel incredibly passionate about your niche, but what you think is a good niche might not be a good niche for blogging success.

Look at the top bloggers and what they talk about. Be smart and think about your topic. You can't talk about toe nail clipping and hope to get a huge following. Think about how many people are interested in your topic. As long as there is a huge following in your industry, and you can always offer great advice about that niche, you have a great chance at earning a nice income as a blogger.

If you don't have a niche or topic right now, you can find a hot topic to blog about and learn to love helping people in that hot topic. You could discover that reaching out to help people will really turn you on, and then you will end up loving what you do. Keep that in mind.

There is a real "high" you will get when helping people, no matter what you do to help them. When you know you are making a difference in other people's lives, there will be a great satisfaction in that process. With that said, you could actually create a blog about teaching people how to make money blogging, just like Michael Dunlap and many other bloggers do. You could also learn to enjoy that process, especially when the money starts coming in.

There are lots of ways to determine what niche is right for your new blog, but we can make the process even easier. In this article, we'll show you exact steps you must take to choose the right niche when you create a new blog.

1. Brainstorm your topic

Without thinking about anything else, start your niche decision process by writing down all the things that interest you. These can be personal interests or professional interests.

Start by thinking about the things you enjoy doing, or would enjoy doing if you had the chance. For example, you are an amateur photographer. Photography blogging could be a great niche. You can share your photos, your detailed knowledge, or your experience with camera technology.

Next, think about the things you would enjoy learning. For example, you're interested in taking up cooking classes. Even if you don't have the time or budget to start cooking classes, you can start up a food blog where you analyze recipes you find online. And discuss how to choose perfect ingredients, and weigh the benefits of organic versus GMO ingredients.

Finally, think about the things you are already diving deep into. For example, let's say that you are an adult that is going back to finish your degree in college. You're going to do a lot of research on on-campus versus online degree programs, what university to choose, how to get back into the swing of studying, and so on. These are great topics for a niche blog about higher education.

During this exercise, you will get a better feeling for the themes that resonate with you. The ones that you are most passionate about are the best candidates for your niche. Also, read this post to understand what types of blogs exist on the web. Whether you are excited about one niche idea or several of them, list them down. Next, we will show you a 3 step formula to confirm your niche for success.

Blog success validation

Whether you want to blog for prestige, income, fun or connections, you'll want to research the niche you choose and make sure the topic is viable. The following "blog success validation" exercise will help you determine if your blog has a real potential. It will also help you understand why 90% of blogs fail.

1. Potential niche size

Even if you believe it's a brilliant blog idea, you will likely struggle to succeed unless you find a niche market that attracts enough people. You don't want your niche to be too small or too big.

For example, the size of the "golf" niche is too big and broad with millions of keywords ideas. But if you pursue a niche that is very narrow, such as "plane golf swing drills," the volume of searches would be too small. One niche down from "golf" would be "golf tips" or even deeper down "golf tips for beginners."

Check the size of your niche

Check the top five keywords for your niche topic. Look for at least 10 thousand monthly searches combined for the five keywords. You can use Google Keyword Planner (free), SERPs tool (free) or WordTracker (freemium) to check for the volume of searches and get keywords ideas. You want to be certain there is a large enough audience looking for the kind of information you will provide. But it shouldn't be too large that you will get lost in the crowd.

With the Google Keyword Planner tool you can get top keyword ideas. However, it won't give you exact numbers of search volume and only the interval of common searches. This information will give you a rough idea of keywords and search volumes. Thus, we suggest using Google to get keywords ideas and other tools to get average search volumes for specific keywords.

If you want to get precise search volume use SERPs tool. Enter your primary keyword (for example use "golf tips") and get ideas by looking at the list of suggested keywords. Select the top five keywords that fit the niche topic you picked. Check the search volume for each keyword and add them together.

For example, applying this search process to our five golf-tip keywords, yielded the following search results:

✓ "golf tips" – 6,600

✓ "golf swing tips" – 6,600

✓ "golf putting tips" – 1,000

✓ "golf tips for beginners" – 880

✓ "golf tips driving" – 880

With these five keywords, we have a little over 20,000 average monthly searches. This niche market ("golf tips") has enough volume and would be a good choice for a blog.

2. Potential competition

It's a good sign if you have competition. It means others are talking about your niche and pursuing it. It's also important to note that bloggers in your niche are not always your competition. And you will have to get to know them sooner or later through your blogging journey.

Following is a competition review process you can use:

- ✓ Do a Google search for "[niche] blog" or "best [niche] blogs." Can you find blogs currently targeting your niche? Are there at least five popular blogs focused on your topic? Don't lose interest if you see a large number of blogs in your niche. If they can do it, so can you!

- ✓ Go to Facebook and do a search for [your niche]. Are there active Facebook pages? Not all topics lend themselves to Facebook, but most do. Look for Facebook pages and see how many followers they have. Great niches will exhibit at least 1,000 fans.

- ✓ Go to Twitter and do a search for [your niche]. Are there active Twitter accounts? You should find many references to your niche on Twitter. Check Twitter accounts of people involved within your niche. See how many followers they have (should be at least 1,000).

Are there offline magazines? This is the gold standard for a niche. If someone is going to the trouble of creating a paper magazine centered on your niche, you can be sure online fans are looking for that information. You can check Amazon Magazines or just do google search for "[your niche] magazine or journal." In regards to our "golf tips" example, this was a no-brainer, we see all the golf-related magazines at the local grocery stores. If one or two of these points are positive, it's a good sign your niche has a potential.

3. Potential monetization

Do you want to earn money with your blog? Many people start blogging as a hobby without looking at monetizing their blog. But, others want to make extra cash or even dream of making a living by blogging. It doesn't matter which category is yours. It wouldn't hurt to know if your blog can produce the income you desire. If you found other blogs, active social profiles and offline magazines in the previous sections, this indicates the niche is alive and monetizable.

To make sure your niche is monetizable, research the following:

✓ Is anyone selling information or products related to your niche? The easiest way to determine this is to see what your competitors are promoting.

✓ Are well-known advertisers in your niche? These could be the big brands or e-commerce sites.

✓ Are there affiliate offers in your niche? Here is how to find affiliate offers: Check affiliate networks (Clickbank.com, CJ.com and ShareSale.com and Amazon Affiliate).

✓ Do a Google search for "[your keyword] affiliate" or "[your keyword] affiliate program."

These points can help you determine if you can establish a blog in the niche of your choice that helps you generate income.

Making the final decision

Now that you've done a validation process for all topics that you had listed. You should have a clear idea of the size, competition, and monetization potential for each subject. And it's time to narrow down your niches.

If you ended this exercise with one niche in mind, then you're ready to go and can start your new blog.

If you are excited about several niches, you might feel like you want to create a blog about them all at the same time. The best approach, yet, would be to focus on one at a time. This way, you can create a solid blog strategy and improve upon it by exploring new topics later on.

VERDICT

Don't jump into niche-specific blogging without a plan. Make sure your niche choice is something that you will want to stick with for years to come. With personal interest, interest from others, and ability to create revenue, your niche blog can become a successful venture!

Chapter Three
How To Build And Monetize Your Blog

You are writing and publishing powerful and informative blog articles a few times a week. You are very careful to write about what others need and want within your area of expertise. How do you monetize your blog?

Do you really want to monetize your blog?

The first question that you need to answer is whether you really want to monetize your blog. There are some people who believe that turning your blog into a money-making tool is not right. Of course, in order to get people to pay attention to what you are doing and subsequently get them to buy what you are selling, there has to be some promotion of your business involved. The idea that social media (which includes blogs, of course) succeeds on the premise of people forming and maintaining relationships and not on hard selling is contrary to monetizing.

Once you have worked out your feelings regarding the ethics and comfort level of monetizing your blog, there are some steps to follow, which will help you to accomplish what you set out to do. You must be committed to making it happen and to jumping in with both feet. For example:

Advertising: If you decide to advertise your blog, you should do it wholeheartedly and really put up as many ads as you feel are appropriate. Don't merely place a tiny advertisement in a far off corner.

Donations: If you want to go the donations route, don't just put in a link for donations and leave it at that. A large number of your visitors may fail to even see the link.

Selling your products and/or services: If you plan to generate income by using your blog to help you sell your products and/or services, make sure that you have something unique and high quality to sell. You need to sell them in a way that compels your clients and prospects to really want to buy.

Expect criticism: When you begin to monetize your blog (if it was free before), you should expect that some of your connections won't like the idea. Hopefully, the majority of the feedback that you will be receiving will be positive. If that is the case, you are still ahead. There will always be people who don't deal well with change. Even those people who offer negative criticism will do so only once or twice, and with any luck, will stop after that.

Will you be able to live comfortably from what you earn with your blog?

The answer to that is most likely yes, if you do it the right way. If you are devoting all of your time to the blog and generating income, you will succeed. If you are working at it part time in addition to having another full time job, it will take longer for you to see results. This doesn't mean that it can't be done. It certainly can be done.

Is generating an income from a blog something that anyone can do?

No, it isn't. In fact, the statistics say that the majority of people who attempt to earn a living from their online work do not succeed. If you are very intelligent about it and go about it the right way, you will succeed. You must apply your intelligence when it comes to your blog to the web itself. You much be web savvy. If you are web savvy, you have a great chance at bringing in money.

What exactly does it mean to be web savvy?

You don't need to have a heavy technical background but you do need to have some knowledge of several different web technologies. The specific list of important web technologies for you and your blog really depends on what you are doing. There are some technologies that are useful for all businesses, such as:

- ✓ HTML/CSS

- ✓ Blog software

- ✓ Trackbacks

- ✓ RSS/syndication

- ✓ Blog comments (and comment spam)

- ✓ Full versus partial feeds

- ✓ Search engines

- ✓ Search engine optimization (SEO)

- ✓ Page ranking

- ✓ Social bookmarking

- ✓ Tagging

- ✓ Traffic analytics

✓ Email

If you don't have acquaintanceship in those areas mentioned, your chances of success will go way down. It is well worth the investment of time and effort to educate yourself before you attempt to do anything as far as monetizing your blog. You will work hard in your efforts but you will also be rewarded for those efforts.

- **Embrace change**

You might now ask yourself what are the risks involved in this venture? The greatest risk that you will be faced with is the idea that opportunities will present themselves and you will miss them. It is critical that you think like an entrepreneur rather than an employee. The thing that is in the strongest position to hurt you is not knowing what you don't know. A very important skill to develop is the ability to recognize opportunities when they come along. If you miss opportunities, you are losing money, you are losing (or not gaining) website traffic and you are losing the chance to help more people to solve their problems.

- **Your income-generation strategy**

You should map out your strategy before you begin and have a philosophy in place. It isn't necessary to write an entire business plan before you begin, however, you need to write a description of how you plan to earn money. Of course, as you continue to grow and succeed, your end number will increase. Once you have started to earn an income from your blog, you will see that there is a lot more security in that than there is if you were working for someone else. Going forward, you should refer back to your income-generation strategy whenever you are faced with the need to make decisions regarding your blog business. It may be helpful to you if you research how other people have designed their strategies and borrow the concepts from them. Nobody ever said that you have to reinvent the wheel.

- **Generating traffic**

The single most important element when it comes to the success of your blog is website traffic. The reason that traffic is so important to your success is that the more people who pay attention to you and what you are offering, the more money you will earn because there are more people who will be willing to pay. The more website traffic you have, the more opportunities you will have.

- **Building traffic**

The way to build traffic is with high-quality and compelling content. Your content needs to be informative, educational, and extremely valuable to your readers. If you don't see a pattern of increase in your traffic month after month, there is a distinct possibility that you are not doing enough. Your strategy may be appropriate and spot on but you may need to be doing more of the same. Your traffic should be increasing with every month that passes by.

The following list is a collection of many of the different ways of making money with your website. Depending on what your website is about, a large number of these techniques can be implemented to earn you cash. But don't get disheartened if one method doesn't work for you just try a different one and build upon that!

I hope this list helps you to see the variety of ways that you can begin to earn money online.

1. Pay Per Click Advertising

You can probably guess from the name how you monetize your blog from this method. You get paid for every click a visitor makes on these ads. You sign up to a provider and they give you a code for you to place on your site. The provider will then send contextual ads to your site (either image or text based) that are relevant to the content of your website. Google AdSense is the most widely used provider of this service, but there are many others out there.

Pay Per Click (PPC) ads vary in profitability depending on the amount of traffic your website gets. Only a small percentage of people will click on these ads, so to earn a lot of money from them you will need a lot of traffic.

The click-through rate (CTR) of your visitors depends on the design of your website. Certain parts of your website pages are more valuable than others, so to increase your CTR these PPC ads can be placed there. For example, space at the beginning and end of articles/blog posts are highly visible, so by putting a PPC in these positions may increase the chances of someone clicking on one. If on the other hand you place these ads at the bottom of the page where nobody can see them, then nobody will click on them.

The cost per click (CPC) can also determine how much you are likely to earn from this type of ad. Adverts that display financial products or mortgages will generate you more income due to the higher price of the actual product, compared with perhaps children's toys. The former may pay you as much as $1+ for every click through by one of your visitors, whereas a click on toys may pay you only a few cents.

Which ads shows up on your site is dependant on the content of your website. After all, it would be daft showing financial products on a website that talks about children's toys and vice versa. PPC ads are a good way to easily monetize your blog. However, to make serious money from them you will need lots of traffic.

You can find PPC adverts for your website at these popular sites:

✓ Google AdSense

✓ Chitika

✓ Clicksor

✓ BidVertiser

2. Cost Per Mile Advertising

Cost per Mile advertising (CPM) is similar to PPC advertising, however, instead of getting paid on a per-click basis, you get paid according to the number of impressions (page views) you get. This is worked out for every 1000 impressions. For example, a website that gets 200,000 page views per month that displays a $1 CPM ad will generate you $200 a month!

There are a number of different CPM providers out there that you can get ads from. Each varies on how much they will pay you, generally the better the provider the higher rate you will be paid. This is because the best providers have access to more and better quality advertisers that are willing to pay you more.

Just like PPC, CPM adverts can pay you more depending on where the advert is placed on your website. The higher the ad is placed and the bigger the ad is, will generally make you more money.

CPM adverts are beneficial for websites that have lots of traffic and a high page view per visitor ratio, but it is still a good option to consider when looking to monetize your blog.

3. Text Link Ads

This type of advertising allows you to place text based ads within the text of your articles. For example, if you are writing an article about a certain software, you can place text-link ads within your posts that would refer your viewers to that particular product.

You can't just link to anything though, you need to sign up to that specific product affiliate advertising scheme (see '10. Affiliate Marketing' below) or you can sign up to a specialised provider who will automate the service.

Text-Link-Ads are quite good as it offers a non-intrusive way to monetize your blog that won't put off your readers.

4. In-text Ads

Very similar to the above text link ads, 'In-text ads' are adverts that are placed inside your text content such as articles or blog posts. You can sign up to an In-text advertising provider that will place sponsored links within your text. These are double underlined to make them stand out from other links, so that when a user moves the mouse over one of them a small advertising pop-up will appear. The user can then decide if they want to click on it, which will make you a small amount of money.

These types of ads are a bit more obvious than the previous type, which can put some people off. If used properly, they can be a good way to monetize your blog.

5. Advertising Widgets

This method is relatively new on the scene. An increasing amount of people are using widgets on their websites to generate some money. These widgets are designed so that they can be easily placed onto a website without any hassle, which display a mixture of PPC, text link ads and affiliate programs.

6. Advertising Space

You can monetize your blog by selling space on your website for advertisers to display a banner. This can be a very lucrative method as it allows you to cut out the middleman and charge what you want for other people to advertise on your site.

Generally these deals are worked out so that you display an ad for a fixed amount of time for an agreed fee with the advertiser. The downside of this method is that you need to commit time to manage the whole process with the advertiser and that your site needs to have a lot of traffic to be considered by advertisers.

7. RSS Adverts

If you have an RSS feed (which you should!) then you can follow in the footsteps of millions of other website owners and start placing ads on it.

Many RSS feed generators now offer this service, so that it is even easier to implement them. Some offer CPM or PPC advertising, however you could opt to do it yourself and offer to sell sponsored messages or banners directly on your feed.

You can find adverts for your RSS feed on BidVertiser that you can implement to monetize your feed, though Google FeedBurner lets you do this as well.

8. Audio Advertising

Something that you may not have even considered, Pay per Play (PPP) are audio adverts that are played every time someone visits your website. The ads usually only last a few seconds, with the viewer unable to stop it. This creates a 100% conversion rate with unique visitors, so you get paid about $5 per visit, however this method is very intrusive and may turn off your visitors, making them less likely to make a return visit.

Another form of audio advertising that you could use is 'Podcast ads'. If you run a podcast on your website, perhaps a weekly update letting your listeners know everything that is new on your website, then you could choose to include advertising. I believe that this type is less intrusive than the former because your podcast would just seem like a short radio show with commercial breaks. As long as you don't go overboard with the amount of adverts, then this may be a method that could use to monetize your blog.

9. Pop-ups/Lightboxes

No doubt that you have heard of these! Pop-ups are very common online, but they are also very annoying. Many people hate pop-ups and have pop-up blockers installed to stop them. However, if executed in the right way, they can work. Having a single pop-up on your website that only appears to new visitors may work. They grab the attention of the visitor on their first visit and after that they won't be bothered again by them.

Pop-ups don't necessarily need to sell products directly. You can use them indirectly to promote aspects of your website, for example PopUp Domination can be used to encourage people to sign up to your email list of tutorial course, or alternatively you can create a lightbox with AWeber.

Pop-ups can work if you make them less annoying to people. The more frequently they appear, the less traffic you will get coming back!

10. Affiliate Marketing

If done right this, method is a great way to monetize your blog. Many of the previous methods can be used as affiliate marketing methods, but often a review of a product can work just as well.

For example, if you have a gardening website you could research affiliate programs that contain products related to gardening. Perhaps someone wants people to advertise their new lawnmower product, you could write a blog entry 'What's the best lawnmower for my garden?' and at the end you could promote the affiliate product.

With this type of advertising, you can get a commission with every sale that resulted from your recommendation. You refer viewers from your site via recommendations, banner ads, text link ads, etc., which takes them to the product page. If they buy, then you get a commission. This is often worked out on a percentage of the sale price, maybe 10-20%, sometimes more (I've seen products offer 75% commission) depending on the individual product.

11. Product Reviews

Basically the same as Affiliate Marketing, but more obvious. You can write detailed reviews about products and publish them on your site. Obviously it is better to review products that are related to your website, as you are catering to your target audience. There is no point writing a detailed review about a solar panel for your roof, if your website is about scuba diving.

Many people can build a website solely around product reviews, writing about a variety of subjects such as, hotels, holidays, cars, gadgets, films, etc. If that product has an affiliate program, then you can make quite a bit of money from it.

12. Create & Sell Your Own Product

We are a society of consumers! If you have a product that you have made, then why not sell it on your website. Perhaps you are a software programmer and have designed an app to help people track stocks on their mobile phone. You could let people download it from your website for a small fee. Maybe your hobby is pottery and you want to sell off some of your work, then sell it on a website. If they are popular, there might be a full-time business for them!

The good thing about this is that compared with selling a product in a shop that has a small customer basis, online you have the world to sell your product to.

13. Write an eBook

Everybody seems to be writing an eBook these days, so why don't you give it a try? These have become very popular in the last few years with the introduction of commercial eReaders such as the Apple iPad and Amazon Kindle.

You could write an eBook about almost anything. Maybe you are good at DIY, you could write a book about renovating your house that people might find useful. You can then sell it through the Apple iStore or on Amazon.

You can sell it directly on your website as well! This way you get 100% of the sale price and you get traffic to your website. Selling your own eBook can be an excellent way to monetize your blog!

14. Write a Hardback Book

This could be a continuation from writing an eBook. If you are a good writer you could publish your book in Hardback or paperback form. You could sell this on your website and send a copy to buyers.

This method is usually only successful for authors that have an existing following. An author may have a successful book that they then build a website around to promote it to a global audience. It can work the other way however. Many people have built a successful blog first and then written a book that has sold well.

If you are a good writer then this could be a good option for you. You can then find a self publishing site, such as iUniverse that lets you publish your very own book.

15. Write Tutorials & Guides

The internet is a great place to find information. Everyone searches for tutorials detailing how to do something. You are reading a guide yourself on '30 ways your website can earn you money' right now!

I myself know very little about cars, so I would find tutorials and guides useful explaining technical things that I don't know. For example, a guide listing 'Help on buying a new car' or 'How to service your own car' would be very useful.

Everybody knows something that they could teach to another, so why not write about it and publish it on your own website. If it's a particularly popular niche that you are writing about, then you could attract a lot of traffic!

16. Teaching Program

The next step from writing tutorials would be to create an online teaching course. You could charge people a membership fee (see #22) or a fixed amount for joining a course that you have set up. These courses could be about anything and could include podcasts, videos, tutorials, etc.

For example, you may be an expert photographer. You could set up a 2 week online training course detailing how to be a better photographer. You could make videos describing all of the different equipment that you might need, techniques that help achieve excellent quality photos, how to develop photos in a dark room, etc.

You need to make sure that the information that you offer to your paying customers is different to any free content that you offer on your site. You will receive a lot of complaints if you just charged people $100 for information that they just read in your free blog! You can only charge people premium prices for premium content.

17. Live Workshops

The next step from creating an online teaching course is to

have a live workshop. Live workshops let you interact with your audience and find out what they like about your website. People who come to your workshops get to meet you and ask you questions face-to-face.

Many people find these types of workshops appealing as they can get so much more out of it, than just following an online tutorial. This is why some people are prepared to pay a lot of money to attend these workshops.

As well as charging people for a ticket, you can make money in other ways from these gatherings. You can promote your own products or books (See methods #12, #13 & #14) at the end of each workshop. If you invite guest speakers to attend your workshops, then you can also collect 50% of everything that they make from promoting their own products.

You can also record the whole event and upload it to your website afterwards, perhaps advertising a future workshop.

Workshops aren't hard to arrange. Many hotels have conference rooms that you can book for an event. Once booked, you have a date to promote to your readers of when the workshop is taking place. You just have to prepare some kind of presentation, and keep advertising your upcoming workshop.

18.Host A Webinar

Webinar's are basically a live workshop online. People go on to Webinar's to hear you talk about your specialist subject. This is great for people that live over-seas that can't get to one of your workshops.

You make money from Webinar's by charging an individual

for a virtual seat on your presentation. They pay to watch you perform your presentation online and they can interact during the process.

Webinar's can incorporate power point presentations, web-cams, photos, microphones, polls, etc., making them fully interactive with your audience. Questions are usually left till the end of the Webinar, where each viewer has the opportunity to ask any questions that they want to you.

You don't have to charge your audience anything to view a Webinar that you are conducting. You could just use it as a marketing tool promoting your website, but the majority of people often host an initial Webinar for free and then charge people for the subsequent ones.

19. Be a Consultant

You could monetize your blog by offering consultancy in your specific niche. You need to have a large number of followers and have built a good reputation in your field for this method to earn you money. You can offer one-on-one consulting to people over the phone or via Skype for a fixed rate. People would be willing to pay a premium for this service as they are paying for your undivided attention for an hour or more.

For example, you have built a reputation as being an expert in health and fitness and have a successful blog talking about methods of weight-loss and healthy eating. You could offer a consultancy service, where for one hour a day people can arrange to talk to you via web-cam to plan out a personal tailored exercise regime. You might charge $100 for the hour and the individual might not need to contact you until the next month.

As previously stated, you do need a reputation for this to generate you any money. This is not a method for a start up website, but it could be something to aim for in the future as you grow your website.

20. Find Sponsors For An Event

If your website involves organising events, such as a workshop (See Method #17), or a weekly podcast, etc., you could find companies to sponsor them. Then at the beginning and at the end you would have to promote the sponsor. You see this type of advertising a lot on TV and in Sport. Many TV shows are sponsored to generate income.

The advantage of this method is that it gives website owners more options to monetise each aspect of their site. Advertisers are attracted to sponsorship deals on high traffic websites as it allows them to reach a targeted audience.

21.Selling Services (Hire Me)

This is often the reason why many people start a website in the first place. You might have a profession in the real world, such as a stock trader, architect, life coach, etc. You could build a website advertising your services to increase your client numbers. Visitors can pay for your professional services through your website and receive your help, as in the previous example this could mean full financial planning and strategies on stock trading.

Obviously, with this method you only get paid when you are working. A great way to find clients is to have your own 'Hire Me' page on your website. That way, people can see that they can hire you to help them out.

22. Membership Site

Increasing numbers of sites offer premium membership areas. The most famous of these are Newspapers who are switching to more online content due to decreasing sales of actual newspapers. Websites attract visitors with free content and then they realise that they can get added benefits by paying a membership fee.

An example of this could be a 3D modelling website. The website could offer free tutorials, detailing step-by-step instructions on how to create 3D renderings of objects, perhaps a car. Paying members can download pre-made 3D models that they can use in animations, etc.

23. Private Forums

Similar to a paid membership, private forums can be created to cater to your audience. Members can pay an annual/monthly fee to access the forum and interact with the other members.

There are many free forums out there, so to charge members a fee to access your forum you need to provide excellent, individual content that isn't available elsewhere.

One example could be a networking forum where people can interact within a professional environment. A forum focusing on academic scientific research could attract scientists from around the world to collaborate with one another.

24. Email Marketing

Email marketing can generate you lots of money. The key is to build a large email list of your customers/visitors. When people register to become a member, you get their email address. When people sign up to your weekly newsletter, you get their email address. The more ways there are to get someone's email address the better.

With an email list, you can build a brand, recommend products, promote any events/workshops that you may be holding and more importantly to can encourage people to keep returning to your website.

Email marketing isn't a direct way of making money, but it is a powerful way of increasing your income from your other methods by driving traffic back to your site. Just don't go overboard with emails so that they are viewed as spam! Nobody likes spam!

Check out this list of software to help manage your email newsletters:

- ✓ AWeber
- ✓ PopUp Domination

25. Surveys & Polls

You can place surveys and polls from certain companies on your website that will pay you for the privilege. You can sign up to these sites and choose a particular survey/poll that will fit in with the content on your website. Visitors of your site can participate in voting, whilst you get paid for displaying it. Most of these polls operate on a Cost per Mile basis.

26. Paid Directory Listings

This method is an alternate way of selling advertising.

Unlike displaying adverts on a page, you allocate space on your website to list links to different companies and services that are related to your niche.

For example, a blog about graphic design could have a separate page that displays links to professional graphic design companies and freelance graphic designers.

You can charge for the privilege to display these links on your website. You can guarantee that the links will be seen by X amount of people per month and you can charge a monthly fee. If you had a list consisting of 500 people and charged them $5 a month, you would make $2500 per month!

27. Job Boards

An advancement of a direct listings is a job board. You can create a web-page that allows companies to post job vacancies. You can charge a small fee for the listing and maybe even a small finders fee if the job is filled by one of your viewers.

This method is very competitive, there are many job boards out there, so a small site will have a very hard time surviving. This could be a suitable method for a larger site, as the more traffic you have, the more listings you are likely to attract.

28. Sell Your Custom Template or Theme

If you have spent time making your OWN custom template or theme, then you can consider selling it. An increasing amount of people are making their own website, therefore there is a demand for more templates.

The amount of money that you can make from this method

depends on your website skills. A high quality template can be sold for as much as $100+ but that is the top of the range themes. If you have a skill for making these then you could build a small business around making and selling them. My website runs on a theme that was purchased. WooThemes is a great place to buy high quality templates.

Donations

A method that a lot of people don't even think of, Donations can provide an alternate source of income from your website. You can get a donate button from PayPal to place on your site and ask people to donate a small amount to you for the service that you provide.

This method is a good way to generate some income if you have a small website, you could ask people to donate an amount to help you pay the upkeep of the website. This method can work for much larger sites as well, generally sites that offer helpful information to its users, can benefit from this method as it allows readers to donate a small amount of money if they feel that you have helped them in some way.

Some people may not like the idea of this, but the advantage of this method is that it can be easily set up and left. If people want to donate anything then they can, if not they don't have to. You'll be surprised how many people are willing to give you some money if you have genuinely helped them.

29. Auction Your Website

Some websites just don't make money for whatever reason, but before you just give up and walk away, you could consider selling your website. You can find many sites that offer to list your site for sale for people to bid on. You would be surprised to see how much some websites can go for.

Why would anybody want to buy your website? Well, that is because people are lazy! It takes time and effort to build a website from scratch, so a lot of people like to buy built websites and build upon them. Some people do it for a living, building websites and then selling them on for a profit.

The advantage of this is that you can make quite a bit of money selling your website, it just depends on the quality of it.

It is a wonderful thing when your blog generates income for you, although it is important to remember that there is a lot of hard work and time involved. It is, of course, very important to stay centered and to keep reasonable expectations. Having a solid, healthy number of followers will be critical to your success as well as all of the other things that were mentioned. You are doing what you love and getting paid for it at the same time. There is no limit to how successful you can be. All people understand that if they want something valuable, there will be times when they have to pay for it and they will be happy to do so. On your end of things, you need to maintain a consistency and a commitment to high quality and value that will make your readers/clients want to be loyal to you and to want to continue to do business with you indefinitely.

How To Build Your Blog To Make Money

With the growth of the World Wide Web, blogging has given a platform and a voice to those of us who may not have had one previously. Blogging will help you get your message out to the public, and you can make money blogging as well.

If you would like to know how to start a blog, here is what you do. Simply do a blog search, and when you find a blog style you like, the homepage will have a link that you can follow to create a blog. After you fill out a short online form, you are on your way to becoming a blogger!

A common beginner blogging mistake is thinking that once you create a blog, viewers and money will start rolling in. Before you learn to blog for money, you should know how to build your blog. The most important thing you can do is post original quality content. When you post your content, always use the spell checker. Proper grammar and spelling will give your blog a more professional look. For more information, do a keyword search for "beginner blogging course" and "beginner blogger products."

Now that you know how to blog, you will need to get some readers. The best way to do this is to visit other blogs, and post quality comments on them. The authors and readers of the other blogs will see your comments, and they may visit your blog and post a few comments themselves. Posting on message boards and forums are also a way to advertise your blog. When you do this, search out message boards that share a common interest with your blog, and offer a link. (If you visit a blog about stamp collecting, and you post a link to a blog post about how to grow tomatoes, you might get banned for spamming.)

Building a good-sized readership is important if you are going to build blogs for money. The more readers you have, the more money you can make. There are many paths to becoming a big time money blogger. One way you can make money with your blog is by using contextual ads. Contextual ads scan your post for content, and automatically put up links to products they think your readers might be interested in. When a reader clicks the ad, you make money. The amount of money ranges from a few cents to a few dollars, but these can build up after time. Contextual ad companies have the blog tools and blog software you need to maximize profits.

A more profitable way to make money blogging is to join a network that will give you access to advertisers who will pay you to post about their products. The more popular your blog is, the more money advertisers are willing to pay you for your posts. (I've seen some that pay as much as $75 dollars for a 200-word post!) If you go this route, remember that you must still post non-advertisement quality content on your blog, and you must continue to advertise your blog for maximum profits.

Now, let's dive into the first step of how to start a blog for beginners.

1. Pick your blog's name

First, it's time to pick a name for your new blog. We'll also select the blogging platform and web hosting you'll be using and in order to get your blog online.

The combination of blogging platform & web hosting I personally use (and that most other bloggers use) is a WordPress blog, hosted by Bluehost. WordPress is a publishing platform that's been around since 2003 and now powers more than 60% of all blogs on the Internet. And Bluehost is one of the longest established companies in the blog hosting industry. This combination is what we'll be using to start blogging with in this guide.

- **Choose your plan**

Next, you'll select a hosting plan. Remember, web hosting is the service that actually gets your blog online and keeps it live on the Internet. Personally, I recommend choosing the Choice Plus plan (which I use)—because it comes with Domain Privacy, which will protect your personal information (your full name, email address, phone number and home address) from being published anywhere online. Instead, Bluehost will guard that information on your behalf.

Choosing your plan will look like this right here. Just click the green "Select" button on your plan of choice:

As I said above, I recommend choosing the Choice Plus plan, so that you're getting the Domain Privacy feature that'll protect your personal information online, but any of these plans will do as you're starting your blog—and you can add the domain privacy in later during the checkout process for around $1/mo.

- **Pick your blog's domain name**

Next, you'll get to the page where it's time to choose the domain name for your blog:

Once you get to this step in the checkout process, just type in the name of the domain name that you'd like your blog to have (mine is ryrob.com).

If your domain name of choice isn't available, you can either try another option that comes to mind—or (what I recommend) select the option to choose your domain name later after getting the rest of your account squared away and taking a little more time to think the name through. Plus, later in this free guide to start blogging, we talk more about how to choose the right name for your blog if you're not yet decided.

Here's where you can click to choose your domain later (it's a popup that will appear if you hover on this page for long enough or move your mouse up toward the top of the page):

After either choosing your domain name or opting to select it later, you'll be taken to the final step in the sign up process—creating your account.

- **Create your Bluehost account**

Start by filling in your account details like your name, email address (it's super important to use an up-to-date email address because this is where your login details and account information will be sent) and address. If you don't want to enter your information manually, you can connect your Bluehost account with your Google account.

- Select the right hosting package

This is where you'll choose an account plan based on the price you want to lock in and how far in advance you'll pay.

Note that Bluehost only offers options for you to pay 1, 2, 3 or 5 years upfront. They don't offer a monthly payment option (because most hosting companies that do offer monthly payments tend to charge a lot more). Even still, with whichever plan you choose, the price works out to be a good deal for starting your own blog and getting it online today.

<u>Which pricing plan is best to start a blog with?</u>

Personally, I recommend choosing the "Prime 36 Month Price" if you want to lock in the lowest possible price for your hosting. That's what I use. And it secures your blog hosting at their lowest rate (and gets you domain privacy) for the next 3 years. And because this low pricing for new customers only applies to the first payment you make, if you were to choose the 1-year plan, your pricing may go up after that first year.

That's why if you choose the 36-month plan, your pricing will be locked in at this rate for 3 years. For that reason, I recommend going with the longest duration plan that your budget can spring for.

- **Choosing the right package extras (skip all but one)**

I highly recommend keeping the Domain Privacy Protection extra, but you can get away with skipping the rest. Later on in this guide, I'll show you the many free and cheap plugins & tools you can use for things like SEO optimization, rendering most of these package extras not necessary.

As I mentioned earlier though, having the domain privacy extra keeps all of your personal contact information (your name, email, phone number and address) private. Now, if you chose the Choice Plus Plan on the previous screen, then your Domain Privacy Protection will be listed as "Free" just like this screenshot above shows—it's included in that plan.

If you chose a Basic or Plus Plan, then you'll want to check the box to add Domain Privacy Protection to your order for around $1/mo. The total you'll now see is the amount you're going to pay today. Remember though, you won't have to pay again for 1, 2, 3 or 5 years depending on the package you chose. Plus, there's a 30-day money back guarantee in case things don't go as planned with your blog.

- **Enter your billing information**

Now you'll input your billing information, check the box that you agree to Bluehost's Terms of Service and then hit the green "Submit" button!

How to pick the right name for your blog

I get a lot of questions from readers about how to name a blog the right way, so I wanted to touch on that a little more here.

If you're not yet sure about what to name your blog, fear not. When you get started with a hosting company like Bluehost, they'll let you choose the domain name later. As I said above, if you don't immediately see the domain name you want available, don't get hung up—just select their option to choose it later after getting everything else set up (remember, execution is what you're here for, not perfection).

But because this is one of the most frequently asked questions I get from readers who are learning how to start a blog, let's dig into this for a moment.

Now, while the name you choose is one of the more important parts of setting up your blog, remember that it's something you can always change in the future—so don't let this step hold you back. Just choose something that's close to the topics you're planning to blog about, or you can even grab yourname.com or yournickname.com (like I've done with my blog here, ryrob.com) and let's keep moving.

Your blog name is the first thing people see when you show up in search results and can often tell them about who you are, what you're writing about, and even your personality.

Like I said, there are tons of ways to come up with a name for your blog (you can even use your own name—or a nickname like me After learning how to pick a niche to blog about, the first thing you want to do is get familiar with other people in your industry (if you're not already).

For example, if you want to start a blog about hiking and you live in the state of California... one name you might consider for your blog could be letshikecalifornia.com (what I chose for my 30 day business idea validation challenge). Check out the other blogs in your niche and pay special attention to how they name and brand themselves.

Is there anything you can learn from, play off of, or subvert? Don't just think about the biggest bloggers in your niche, but look for fresh inspiration and things that stand out to you.

You can even get a little outside your niche and look for words that some of your favorite companies use. I like to call this looking for "good words." What words keep popping up that you're drawn to? Make a list of these.

Next, identify the message you want to deliver by choosing to start a blog

You're learning how to start a blog for a reason, and a powerful name for your blog may be sitting at the core of your desire. Go back to your list from picking a blog niche and start to dig into what represents the core message you're trying to communicate. As Nate Weiner, founder of Pocket said:

"The first question to ask yourself is why do you want to rebrand? What does your company and product mean? Where do you want to take it into the future? Does your existing or new name let you do that?"

This might feel like a big question, but don't let it paralyze you. A great name has meaning, but there are plenty of good ones that are just plain fun and memorable.

Now, put yourself in your reader's shoes

You've laid some good groundwork, but now it's time to get serious. Think about your future blog's general topic area and who your ideal reader is. What do they want to read? What's going to grab their attention? What's going to tell them they have to read your blog?

Start with a list of everything you want your blog to be about. Go deep. There are no bad ideas here. Once you've got a massive list, start to look for connections and combinations that might work. Try to keep them simple and memorable.

Some great blog name examples are:

- ✓ Art of Manliness
- ✓ Smart Passive Income
- ✓ Epicurious
- ✓ The Huffington Post
- ✓ Learn to Code with Me

✓ Finally, say the name of your blog out loud and tell it to others

It's easy to get wrapped up in some fun wordplay when it comes to picking a blog name.

But it still needs to be easy enough that people will remember it and be able to tell their friends about you. To practice, say the name out loud and to friends and family. What do they think about it? What emotions does it bring up for them?

They might not be your ideal reader, but they can still give you a good outsider's perspective either way.

And if you're still struggling to come up with a novel name for your blog, try one of these domain name generators that can help come up with some more creative ideas for naming your blog today.

2. Get your blog online (web hosting)

However, if you want to go with a web hosting provider other than Bluehost to secure your blog's name & domain, you'll till need to set that up before moving forward.

Again, I don't want this to feel overwhelming, so let's get the basics out of the way:

What is web hosting?

I touched on this a bit in step #1 above, but to make your website accessible to other people on the Internet, you need a "host." The host keeps all your website files safe, secure and makes sure that people can access your blog when they click on a link or type in your URL.

I use and recommend Bluehost to every blogger, because it acts as a one-stop shop for great (affordable) web hosting and quick & easy registration of your domain name in one swoop. And if you already followed everything in step #1 above, then you've got Bluehost set up to be your web hosting provider so no need to worry

If you're committed to learning how to start a blog that can eventually make money (the way I recommend you doing it), nothing gives you the security, features, and peace of mind that your blog will be up when you need it to be like Bluehost does.

That being said, there are a other web hosting providers worth considering for new bloggers:

The 2 best alternative blog hosting platforms worth considering

Dreamhost — I've hosted literally dozens of websites on Dreamhost over the years (and I still do). All similar features like 1-click WordPress install, free SSL certificate and site security aside, one of the biggest pros of going with Dreamhost compared to other hosting companies, is that they offer a true pay-per-month plan that allows you to pay for the cost of your blog hosting each month with no strings attached. Here are a few other web hosting companies that also offer monthly payment plans.

Namecheap — The thing that sets Namecheap apart from other hosting companies, is their domain marketplace. You can still register a brand new domain name with them, but if you'll also find thousands of domain names that have already been registered and are now for sale—often a good way to acquire a site that has some existing domain authority to jump start your ability to rank content in search engines.

If you still want to evaluate more of the top blog hosting providers, then head on over to my breakdown of the ten best web hosting plans for bloggers this year.

Now we're at the point in this guide where everything from here on out will be built upon the assumption that you've already registered your domain name and chosen the right hosting plan—so if you haven't done so already, take just a few minutes to quickly get set up on Bluehost.

3. Design your blog with a free WordPress theme

Now that you've gotten through the first phase, it's time to get into the fun part of how to start a blog.

Designing your WordPress blog is when you might start to feel a little friction with the process of starting a blog (if you've never done this before), but I promise this won't get too technical.

❖ Choosing the best (free) WordPress theme for your blog

I don't necessarily recommend buying a paid WordPress theme like the one I use (OptimizePress) as a new blogger, until you have some traffic and are generating at least a little income from your blog. While OptimizePress is an incredible theme, diving into something like that at this stage will be a distraction from your most important priority of actually bringing readers to your blog.

WordPress comes with a ton of free themes to choose from, so start with one of the options you like in Appearance >

Themes > Add New Theme > Popular without spending much time on this for now. You can always come back and change it later.

I recommend going with the free Elementor Page Builder. Once you download the free version of Elementor, you'll get their (amazing) detailed instructions on how to install & optimize the theme too:

I like Elementor so much because it's super crisp, clean, simple and will get you to a good starting point without needing to invest in a paid theme as you just start blogging.

Plus, as your new blog begins to grow, Elementor's upgrade options that unlock more widgets, templates and design resources—is seriously as good as it gets when it comes to the best WordPress themes on the market today.

How to evaluate other WordPress themes for your blog

Picking a theme for your WordPress blog can be a lot of fun. But it can also take up a ton of time that you could otherwise be using to write and promote your posts (and thus getting to your first blog income faster). Here are my recommendations of the 25 Best WordPress Themes for Bloggers.

There are so many themes to check out, that it's easy to get swept away by the ones that look awesome, but might not be functionally great. Remember, design isn't just about how your blog looks. It's about how it works. And the easier it is to navigate and read, the better.

Here are a few suggestions of what to look for when evaluating WordPress themes:

- **Keep it simple:**

At the end of the day, the goal of starting a blog is to share content that can be easily consumed (read, watched, experienced). And unfortunately, a lot of fancy blog themes get in the way of that. Don't get too drawn in by crazy looking WordPress themes that compromise on legibility and usability. If a theme looks good, but doesn't help you share your thoughts and engage with readers, it's not a good theme.

- **Responsiveness is a must:**

Responsiveness refers to themes that make sure your blog looks as good on a laptop, as it does on someone's smartphone. Today, more and more people use their phones to read blogs and depending on your audience, that number could be 50% or higher (like mine is). Google also favors mobile-friendly websites and ranks them at the top of their organic search results. If you're not totally sure whether a theme is mobile friendly or not, copy and paste the URL of the theme's demo page into Google's Mobile Friendly Test page. (This test will almost always show some warnings. But major red flags to watch out for are text too small or content wider than screen.)

Does it work in different browsers? Your readers won't just be using different devices, but different browsers. Most theme developers rigorously test their themes across browsers, but sometimes mistakes slip through. Try testing on a couple different browsers just to make sure.

- **Supported plugins:**

If you're using WordPress, the real power of your blog comes from plugins. These are "Add-ons" to your blog that give you extra functionality. Make sure the theme you're choosing supports all popular plugins. If you're unsure, ask the developer.

SEO friendliness: SEO, or search engine optimization, refers to how well Google and other search engines can find your information when people search for it. Some themes use bulky code that makes it difficult for search engines to read. And while no one expects you to inspect a theme's code you should see if the developer has said it is optimized for SEO.

Support: Problems happen. And when they do, you want to be able to ask for help. Lots of free theme developers won't offer support for their products. So that's one thing to be aware of when making your choice.

- **Ratings and reviews:**

Look for themes with a good track record. If the theme is sold on a third-party marketplace you should be able to see reviews no problem. For free WordPress theme, you'll see the ratings just below the download button.

With all of this in mind, my recommendation is to use Elementor as your WordPress theme of choice, as it'll be the best theme for new bloggers to learn on.

Once you've settled on the right theme for your WordPress blog, it's time to dive into the world of WordPress plugins, to help unlock even more customizations and must-do prep work in order to give your blog a strong chance of developing into a full on business.

❖ Pick a WordPress theme for your blog

WordPress is the foundation of your site. There's an easy way to change how WordPress looks without having to code anything yourself.

WordPress uses "themes," little packages of code that can be swapped in and out. Whenever you change your theme, your site will also change. The best part is that your blog post content won't change. This makes it very easy to evolve your site over time without having to rebuild your entire site from scratch.

For now, you'll need to pick your first WordPress theme.

When picking a theme for any of my blogs, I go straight to StudioPress. The themes are a bit more expensive at $130. (Most themes go for $20–50.) In my opinion, the higher price is well worth it. StudioPress was purchased by WP Engine and WP Engine now includes all the StudioPress themes as part of its hosting package. It's a nice freebie if you are already planning on hosting your site with WP Engine.

If you want a wider selection of WordPress themes at standard prices, Themeforest is the most popular WordPress theme marketplace. You'll find just about anything you want in its selection.

After you purchase your theme, log into your WordPress blog, go to the Theme section which is under Appearance in the WordPress sidebar menu. Then follow the instructions for adding the theme. You'll have to upload the theme files to WordPress and activate the theme from within WordPress. You can find the upload option by going to Themes > Add New, a button towards the top. Then you'll see this option to upload:

❖ **Add WordPress Themes**

You'll be able to manage any themes you've uploaded to your WordPress blog from your Themes section:

4. Install your WordPress plugins

Once of the best parts about WordPress is that it's infinitely customizable. Since it's open-source, you can change it to do whatever you want.

WordPress plugins are little batches of software you can install within WordPress to get extra functionality. This is how you'll add a bunch of extra features to your site without having to code anything yourself.

Be careful here and try not to go overboard.

Some bloggers will install dozens or even hundreds of plugins on their blog. That can cause a bunch of problems later on. Not only can plugins cause unexpected conflicts with each other, they become a security liability since it's unlikely that every plugin owner will maintain the plugin over time. They also become a huge headache to manage. When you have that many plugins, you're never sure which plugin is causing a particular problem.

I like to keep my plugins limited to 5–10 amazing plugins. Here are a few of my favorites:

Akismet – Required for every blog, it automatically filters a ton of comment spam which is a problem for every blogger. This is one of the few plugins that I happily pay to upgrade.

Yoast SEO – The most highly recommended SEO plugin, it handles a bunch of SEO tasks automatically for you and also makes on-page SEO tasks a lot easier.

Contact Form 7 – The most popular contact form out there. Set up a contact page on your site and then use this plugin to create a contact form that will email you any time someone fills out the form. Super easy.

TinyMCE Advanced – A bunch of improvements to the WordPress editor that makes writing in WordPress a lot easier. These days, I usually skip this one. I write all my posts in Google Docs and then format them in WordPress using its default HTML editor.

WP Super Cache – A good plugin to speed up your site.

MailChimp for WordPress – More on this below. It's easiest way to connect your WordPress site to a MailChimp account, create an email sign up form, and start collecting email subscribers.

WordPress Popular Posts – Easiest way to add a list of your most popular posts to your blog sidebar. The list will update automatically.

There is a plugin for just about anything you could want to do with your WordPress site. Use the plugin page within your WordPress blog to search for anything that you need.

5. Install Google Analytics

Google analytics is a free website analytics tool from Google. Even though it's free, it's still the best analytics tool out there.

Analytics is just a fancy word for website data.

Yes, analytics can get pretty complicated and overwhelming. Which is why we're going to ignore the majority of what's in Google Analytics for now. All you need to do is create a Google Analytics account and install it on your blog. There are two reasons for this.

First, Google Analytics stores your data over time. When you're ready to dive in later, you'll be thankful that you've been collecting data since the beginning.

Second, it's exhilarating to watch people visit your site in the beginning. I remember the first time Google Analytics recorded a visitor on my first blog. I thought it was a mistake. "Someone visited my site? Really? Why would they do that? Who are they? Did they like it?"

Seeing those first visitors come in will give you a huge motivation boost. Even if you only check Google Analytics to see your total traffic, it's well worth the time it takes to set up.

It's also pretty easy to set up.

6. Set up your email list for the blog

Sooner or later, you'll hear a stat like this:

"Email marketing has 22X the ROI of any other marketing channel!"

Technically, this is true.

The response from email will always dominate any other channel that you try pushing a campaign to. But you have to acquire those emails first. In other words, email by its nature is more responsive, so the comparison ROI stats are kind of dumb. They're stating the obvious.

It's kind of like going to a strawberry field, picking the best strawberries in the entire field, putting them in a gift basket, then declaring that the gift basket strawberries are 12 times as delicious as normal strawberries. Of course they're more delicious — you picked the best ones already!

That's how email lists work. They're a gift basket of the best strawberries. Every marketing engine I've built for companies has relied on emails at its core.

Think of your email list as a giant laser ray you can focus on any offer you want. Selling consulting? Pitch your list. Publishing a new blog post? Pitch your list. A podcast just interviewed you? Pitch your list. Of all the marketing channels that have come and gone over the years, nothing compares to the power of a high quality email list.

Even if you're not sure what to send your email subscribers, that's okay!

Using MailChimp, you can start collecting emails on your blog so that the list is ready for you as soon as you need. It takes time to build a decent size list so your future self will be extremely grateful if you set it up now.

You only need two things:

- ✓ A MailChimp account

- ✓ An opt-in to sign up on your sidebar

MailChimp has a free account for up to 2,000 email subscribers, which will cover your blog for awhile.

Email Optin Example

There's also a super easy WordPress plugin for MailChimp.

Once you install it on your WordPress blog, it'll connect to your MailChimp account and give you an easy way to add an email signup form to your blog sidebar.

Even a super basic opt-in in your blog sidebar like this is enough to get you started:

Don't even worry about sending any emails yet unless you want to. The main thing is that you're collecting email subscribers from the beginning. Email lists can be a gold mine once you have a few thousand subscribers, and the money really rolls in once you have 10,000 subscribers and above.

7. Get into your blog posting groove

Writing blog posts isn't a sprint, it's a marathon. More like a multi-day backpacking trip.

The best bloggers settle into a consistent writing pace they can maintain for a few years. That's right, years.

Here are a few posting frequency rules of thumb:

- At the bare minimum, find a way to post once per week. This needs to be a substantial post, too: 2,000 words at least. I recommend you start here.

- Serious bloggers will post 2–3 times per week.

- Larger sites quickly get to 5–7 posts per week. This requires multiple authors.

- The heavy hitters who push things to the limit will do 25–50 posts per week. No joke, this is for large businesses using content marketing as their primary customer acquisition channel. HubSpot is a classic example of this.

When I look at this chart of blog posting frequency from Orbit Media's survey of more than 1,000 bloggers, I'm not surprised that 21% of bloggers are infrequent or less than monthly. (Let's get real, less than monthly is not regular enough for most readers to know when you'll be posting a new blog.) If you post weekly, you're already posting more regularly than 57% of other blogs — this gives you a huge advantage.

I know writing isn't easy. After writing blog posts full time for three months, I always want to throw my MacBook out the window. It's a grind for all of us. This is why I recommend one post per week. That still gives you the majority of the week to focus on other aspects of your site while also giving you a break from writing blog posts all the time.

A really great post should take you two days to complete. The first day is for research and outlining, along with as much writing as you can complete. The second day is for finishing the writing, proofreading, and publishing the post in WordPress. Also, push quality as hard as you can. The key to building a site and traffic over time is to write posts that are more valuable than what other people have already published in your category.

8. Build an audience around your blog

There's a super famous article in blogging circles: 1,000 True Fans.

Basically, getting 1,000 true fans means you can fully support yourself. You can quit your job, work from wherever you like, and be in complete control of your life.

All from hitting a very reasonable goal of 1,000 true fans.

With blogging, you'll build your audience of 1,000 true fans slowly and consistently. As long as you keep it at, you will get there. Typically, it takes a few years.

Here's what to focus on in order to get there faster:

- Always post at least once per week. Never skip a week.

- Start posting 2–3 times per week if you can.

- On every post, push on quality as hard as you can. Google the topic and see what other people have done, then ask yourself how you can write something even better.

- Write stuff that hasn't been written to death already. Find a new take or perspective on your topics that other people haven't already covered.

- Find your voice and be authentic so people can get to know you. This builds connections with your audience faster. A quick hack for this is to pretend that you're writing your posts to a close friend.

- To push even harder, get active in other online communities. Post in Facebook groups, subreddits, on Twitter, do podcast interviews, get speaking engagements when you can — anything and everything. Be as helpful as you can be in these communities.

- For all of your content, constantly ask yourself, "How can I make this as valuable as possible?"

As your blog audience matures you will want to change your traffic strategies as you grow.

Chapter Four
How To Start Doing Affiliate Marketing With Your Blog

Starting an affiliate marketing blog is actually quite easy. You can start an affiliate marketing blog in just a couple of hours or less. If you set aside an hour or two and follow this step-by-step guide to starting an affiliate marketing blog from start to finish, you will have your very own website all set up and ready to make you some money.

When starting your affiliate marketing blog, it's important to do things in the correct order. Listed below are the steps I recommend you take, and I recommend you do the steps in the exact order that I've laid out.

1. **Step 1: Identify A Niche Market**

Before we get into how to set up your actual blog, you need to identify a niche market that you want your blog to be about. This step can be a bit tricky for the new affiliate marketer because finding a great niche takes a certain kind of balance.

For example, let's say I'm passionate about cars. Well, creating a site just about cars is way too broad. So, maybe I'd focus on classic cars instead. That would be a niche within' a larger market (cars −> classic cars). Heck, I'd probably even drill down deeper and pick a specific type of car like classic Ford Mustangs.

What I recommend is to be very specific and go after what would be called a "micro-niche", but give yourself room to expand later on. For instance, when I'm first starting, I might make my car website about a specific year of the Ford Mustang, like the 1969 Ford Mustang. It could take me months to create content just about the 1969 Ford Mustang, but eventually, I'd likely want to expand the site to include additional models and years.

The point is to be highly relevant to your future website visitors. Say I'm a car guy looking for facts about the 1969 Ford Mustang. Sure, I could read a boring Wikipedia article or an article from some big brand website, but what if I found a website by someone who is so passionate about the 1969 Ford Mustang he created an entire site about it? By doing this, you'll seed your site to gain followers, links, and shares on social media. By the time you're ready to expand, you'll already have a great reputation going for you.

The lesson here is, if you're afraid your niche idea is too narrow, you're probably on the right track. You can always expand later. By narrowing your niche, you have a much better chance of having early success which will serve as motivation to keep pushing.

2. Step 2: Perform Keyword Research

First of all, what is "keyword research?" This is simply researching what people in your target audience search for when they use a search engine like Google. Creating a helpful website is worthless if nobody ever finds it, and most people will find your website by doing Google searches. So, the key here is to create a list of at least 100 "keywords" that people use in search engines.

For example, this page you're currently on right now is specifically created to show up in search results when people search for "how to start an affiliate marketing blog." by doing keyword research, I was able to see that people often type this into Google. I'll show you how to write content to rank for specific search phrases a bit later, but for right now, you just want to make a giant list of these keywords so that you have article ideas that will last you months.

Now, the next question is, how does someone perform keyword research? Well, there are lots of ways, including using expensive "keyword research tools" like LongTailPro.com. My biggest recommendation, however, is to watch the below video and learn how to perform excellent keyword research for free.

3. Step 3: Register A Domain Name

A domain name is simply the URL of your website. For example, the domain name for this website is "AffiliateMarketerTraining.com". Finding a good domain name you like can be a bit tough because most of the "good" domain names are taken. Here are a few tips to consider when registering a domain name:

❖ Only use a .com domain –

I personally only register .com domain names and I recommend you stick with a .com domain as well. There are lots of new extensions you can go with, but still, to this day, nothing is as trusted as a good ol' .com domain.

❖ Make it brandable –

Try to make your domain name brandable. As a personal

example, I have a site DogFoodInsider.com and also created CatFoodInsider.com as well. The eventual plan is to have a whole bunch of "insider" branded domain names in the pet industry.

❖ **Try the "radio commercial test" –**

Your domain name should be easy to say and understand. In order to ensure you have a domain name that is easy to understand, try the "radio commercial test". Pretend your website has a radio commercial and your domain name is said over the radio. Would it be easy to understand? If so, you're on the right path!

❖ **Leave yourself room to expand –**

Previously, I had the example of making a website for classic Ford Mustangs and starting with the 1969 Ford Mustang specifically. I wouldn't want to have a website domain that is specific to the 1969 Ford Mustang because eventually, I'd want to expand the site. Think about where your site will be in 2 or even 5 years from now.

Where Do I Register A Domain Name?

You can register a domain name at any "domain registrar". There must be hundreds if not thousands of domain registrars available, but in this tutorial, we're going to set up web hosting and register your domain name at the same time using the same service. I promise you it will be very easy.

How To Find An Available Domain Name

Before we actually register your domain name, you have to find a domain name you like and one that is actually available. This really is a trial and error process along with your own creative juices. Check out the tool below to search for available domain names, but don't register it yet! Just search for and find an available domain name you like, and we'll get it registered shortly.

4. Step 4: Setting Up Web Hosting

In order to start an affiliate marketing blog, you'll need to have a "web host". Keeping things simple here, but basically, a web host provides you with the ability to actually broadcast your website over the internet. The service I recommend for web hosting is called Bluehost. They are a very well known web host and specialize in people who are new or don't know much about web hosting and building websites. They are also very competitive on price at less than $3 per month. Here is the step-by-step process to set up:

5. Step 5: Choose Your Hosting Plan

For this step, you can choose whatever plan you want, but I reccomend just going with the Basic plan. You can always upgrade later and for your initial needs, the basic plan provides everything you need.

6. Step 6: Enter Your Domain Name

Your Bluehost hosting plan includes domain registration. So, simply enter the available domain name you found earlier. You'll notice a checkbox that says "keep non-house affiliate cookie". Honestly, it doesn't really matter if you check this or not and you can change it later, so don't even worry about it for now.

7. Step 7: Put In your Personal Details

8. Step 8: Enter Your Subscription And

Payment Details

You can choose to pay monthly or yearly, so simply choose your preference. You'll also be asked to enter your payment info.

9. Step 9: Check Your Email

Once you've submitted your payment info, you should get a welcome email from Bluehost. Go ahead and click on "Create your password" to continue your account creation.

10. Step 10: Install WordPress

By now, you probably already know what WordPress is. If you don't, know what WordPress is, basically it is the largest website and blog building platform in the World, and it's totally free. Bluehost has made it really simple to set up a WordPress blog.

First, you'll want to pick a "theme" and choose how your site will look. Don't worry, you can change this later:

11. Step 11: Launch Your Site!

In just one click, you will have your domain name and website live on the internet for all to see!

12. Step 12: Familiarize Yourself With The WordPress Dashboard

This step does take some time. Learning how to use WordPress has a little bit of a learning curve, but you don't need to know any computer code or have technical skills to use WordPress. Simply click around and try to get familiar with how to navigate the backend menus.

13. Step 13: Create Your First Page

The two most important areas of your WordPress dashboard are Pages and Posts. You'll want to use Pages for things like your About Me page, disclaimers, privacy policy, the home page, etc. For day to day articles and content you post on the site, you'll generally want to use posts.

14. Step 14: Create Your First Blog Post

Well, you wanted to learn how to start an affiliate marketing blog and here we are. We're ready to create your very first blog post! If all goes well, this will be your first blog post of hundreds, if not thousands. The video below gives a pretty good tutorial on how to create your very first blog post.

15. Step 15: Find And Apply To Affiliate Programs!

No matter what niche industry you picked, there is always something to promote. Maybe it's a training course from Udemy.com, a company that offers a generous affiliate program. Or maybe it's a digital product you can promote through Clickbank.com. One of the largest and most popular affiliate programs is the Amazon Associates affiliate program.

A word of caution: Don't apply to affiliate programs too early. It's going to take months for your affiliate marketing blog to get enough website traffic that you can truly monetize. Worry about creating high-value content and value to your site visitors first. If you do that, the money will come later.

Congratulations! You Have An Affiliate Marketing Blog!

If you followed all of the above steps, you now have a fully functional affiliate marketing blog. You have a domain name, website hosting, an 'about me' page and your first blog post.

So, what do you do from here? Now that your affiliate marketing blog is all set up, what should your day to day tasks be? At this point, it's all about content, content, and more content.

Remember that keyword research we performed earlier? You should have a list of at least 100 keywords. It's now time to start writing as many articles as you sanely can. If you do this consistently for several months, your efforts will begin to pay off. Most new affiliate marketers get burned out quickly and don't keep at it, but those who do are rewarded. You have to make it past the point where most people fail.

What Are The Main Difficulties

Before we even dig in you already have an idea of what challenges you face daily. Instead of going at it blind, prepare yourself with the tools necessary to take on these common issues head first. You will be so happy you did!

1. Finding a Niche

Problem: Defining where to start is always a challenge, especially if you are new to blogging. A lot of your time is spent finding that topic that really calls to you. When I began I really only had a spark of an idea. Over time I have been able to refine what it is that I actually cover. Here are somethings you could find helpful.

Remember: You must instantly communicate who you are

and what you do as soon as someone lands on your blog. "People make snap judgements. It takes only 1/10th of a second to form a first impression about a person, and websites are no different. It takes about 50 milliseconds (that's 0.05 seconds) for users to form an opinion about your website that determines whether they like your site or not, whether they'll stay or leave.

2. Producing Quality Content

Problem: You have developed a niche that is all your own, written in your own style and voice. Perhaps you even planned ahead and developed a content schedule that covers different facets of your topic equally and systematically over time. However, after several weeks or months of writing you find it difficult to cover new and exciting content.

Remember: You must continue to stay inspired to develop awesome content. Follow your favorite bloggers on Bloglovin', pin your favorite articles on Pinterest and screenshot those inspirational images on Instagram. Review often!

3. Battling the Noise

Problem: There are millions of bloggers in the U.S. and even more around the world. How do you compete in this sea of noise? Not only are people bombarded with other blog content, but hundreds, if not thousands of chance exposures to advertisements and media everyday. Just twenty minutes in Times Square and you could be exposed to over 500 messages. How in the world are you supposed to stand out?

Remember: You do what you do for a reason. It might help

to reflect on why you turned down this path in the first place. I recently did this exercise and not only did it help me, but also my readers began to understand my motivation and purpose.

4. Connecting with Others

Problem: It is very easy to feel like we are on a lonely island in the middle of the deep blue sea, but I promise you are not alone. Creating connections in your niche and/or business are crucial to its survival. But creating these relationships on and offline can be a struggle.

Remember: In the mean time, you really ought to stop "networking" and start creating lasting relationships instead.

5. Monetizing Your Efforts

Problem: You put all this effort into creating content, getting it out there and for what. Well, hopefully, you are planning on getting some kind of return for all that effort. There are tons of articles out there to begin monetizing your site. Everything from adding google ads to your website or using some sort of affiliate marketing.

Remember: If you are strategically trying to monetize your blog, making your readers aware of what you offer needs to be at the forefront.

Chapter Five
Successful Bloggers Who Make Thousands Of Dollars Every Month

There was a time when blogging was considered to be a platform for individual enthusiasts to publish their thoughts, without really being hailed as a money-making job, or a job at all, apparently.

Today, blogging is not just any earning job, it is one of the most coveted and entrepreneurial ways of generating sustained income. Make no mistake though, it is one of those jobs that require utmost dedication, persistence, and some reasonable amount of business sense and capability to scale up. Many people associate blogging with glamor, and it is, but most people fail to see the years and years of hard work and the painstaking long hours that bloggers put into making their blog a powerhouse of quality content and source of income. Content is king, and it stands true for each and every blogger that have made it big.

In this age of internet penetration, with smartphones in every hand, we tend to resort to seeking information on the internet for every little thing in our life. Need fashion advice? Check out the top fashion websites. Stuck with the new tech gadget? Just read the guide on the expert tech blogs. From world news to business advice to arts, there are some fantastic blogs out there providing content of excellent quality. With increasing digital footprints, more and more bloggers are finding ways to monetize their blog through various means, mainly sponsored advertising, with some having struck gold and raking in a colossal amount of income.

Top Earning Blogs In The World

We aren't talking about mere thousands of dollars. We are talking about the big bucks league, 7-figure making blogs! The only thing common among these giants is the ridiculous amount of determination and endurance their owners have shown to build them up.

Without much further ado, let's check out the top 10 highest paid, professional bloggers.

1. Arianna Huffington: HuffPost

Founded in 2005 by Arianna Huffington along with three others, HuffPost, until last year, was The Huffington Post. HuffPost is no short of a legend in the core blogging industry, having started as a platform for politically unbiased and liberal news, among other content. Today, it has sections on news, entertainment, sports, business, technology, arts and many, many more.

Having received funding from the likes of SoftBank Capital earlier, The Huffington Post was sold to AOL in 2011 for $315 million. With an estimated net worth of $1 billion, HuffPost has both local and multiple international editions and makes money by displaying paid advertisements on its website as banners and other digital ads.

While HuffPost ended its practice of publishing the works of unpaid bloggers, which was the initial essence of the site, earlier this year, it has since launched new opinion and personal sections that feature contributions from paid bloggers.

2. Peter Rojas: Engadget

Engadget is a franchise of 10 blogs focused on the technology and consumer electronics domain. It was found in 2004 by Peter Rojas of Gizmodo and was sold to AOL in 2005. It covers exhaustive reviews of new gadgets and electronics and is a go-to site for every gadget enthusiast. Engadget operates ten blogs at present, among which 4 are written in English and the rest are international variants having their own editing team.

Engadget earns more than $5.5 million a month, with advertising as its main source of income. Over the last 14 years, it has established itself as an expert by publishing first-rate content in the form of articles and videos. In 2010, Engadget was also ranked as one of the top blogs by Time magazine.

Its sections include gaming, entertainment, gadget reviews, as well as news and events from around the world, attracting traffic of over 47 million in a month!

3. Rand Fishkin: Moz

Founded by Rand Fishkin as a SaaS company providing marketing analytics tools and subscriptions, Moz is now a fully featured online blog providing its readers' all-inclusive information on search engine optimization and digital marketing. It generates its income from the tools and services it offers its users, including keyword research, site audits, rank tracking and more.

Its blog covers everything about search engine and online marketing and has articles from the industry's top professionals. Earning over $4.5 million in monthly revenue through its blog and SaaS subscriptions, Moz receives more than 6 million traffic hits in a month.

Having raised multiple rounds of funding, including $1.1 million in 2007 in series A, $18 million in 2012, and $10 million in 2016 by the Foundry Group, Moz has established itself as the one-stop shop for all marketers looking for sophisticated tools as well and quality information about search engine marketing.

In February 2018, Rand Fishkin exited the company to start a couple of other initiatives.

4. Michael Arrington: TechCrunch

Focusing on every happening in the technology vertical, TechCrunch is a name synonymous with towering success. Launched in 2005 by Michael Arrington, TechCrunch too, like HuffPost and Engadget, was acquired by AOL in 2010, saying a lot about AOL's acumen and foresight.

Apart from covering and analyzing the tech market trends, dedicatedly profiling tech startups and featuring some of the most prominent names in the industry, TechCrunch is also known for its distinct Disrupt conferences, first organized in 2011 in San Francisco, and now in New York City and Europe as well. The conference promotes a competition for startups, wherein they pitch their ideas to venture capitalists for a sum of prize money.

Available in English, Chinese and Japanese, Techcrunch earns a revenue of over $2.5 million monthly through sponsored banner advertisements and receives over a whopping 31 million in online traffic in a month.

5. Pete Cashmore: Mashable

Founded by Pete Cashmore in 2005 working from his home in Scotland, Mashable is a digital news blog covering everything from technology and science to lifestyle and entertainment. It heavily promotes itself through social media, focusing mainly on Facebook and Twitter.

Recognized by the Time Magazine as one of the 25 best blogs in the world, Mashable was bought by Ziff Davis for $50 million in December last year and has since grown to a revenue of over $2 million monthly and a viewership of over 25 million individual users.

Mashable makes money through different forms of paid advertising while churning out exceptional content on a consistent basis through 6 editions – Mashable Asia, Mashable UK, Mashable Australia, Mashable France, Mashable India and Mashable Global. It also acquired the YouTube channel CineFix to advance its presence in the video domain.

6. Martin Lewis: MoneySavingExpert.com

Covering all topics related to personal finance, MoneySavingExpert.com was founded by the British financial journalist, Martin Lewis, in 2003. The blog features quality-rich content on consumer savings, along with offering its readers various tools like a mortgage calculator, credit card eligibility checker and more, to obtain more information on how they can cut down on their bills.

An established name in the financial domain, the blog does not feature traditional sponsored banner and display advertisements. It generates its revenue by recommending products to its readers and earns commission through those affiliate links.

MoneySavingExpert.com was acquired by Moneysupermarket.com in 2012 and since then has reached a total traffic of more than 30 million in its website, with a monthly revenue of over $1.3 million.

7. Brian Clark: CopyBlogger

Launched in 2006 by Brian Clark, CopyBlogger contains all there is to know about content marketing, and as the name suggests, blogging. Owned by the marketing firm Rainmark Digital, CopyBlogger provides an exhaustive resource center to its readers on online marketing.

It also offers digital marketing tools and services through its parent company, Rainmark Digital, along with training on content marketing. It also has a separate section on WordPress, educating bloggers about hosting and themes.

CopyBlogger is an esteemed blog in the marketing domain, setup illustriously by Brian Clark. It currently clocks over $1 million in revenue through selling its marketing tools and services, hosting approximately 1 million monthly visitors.

8. Perez Hilton: PerezHilton.com

Formerly known as PageSixSixSix.com, PerezHilton.com is a well-known blog in the entertainment domain, publishing content on celebrity gossip. Owned by the media figure Perez Hilton, a.k.a Mario Armando Lavandeira Jr, the blog covers happenings in the entertainment industry.

Lavandeira himself is a TV anchor, a celebrity commentator

and a former actor graduated from the NYU. The content published on the blog is often dubious due to the biases of its creator, which has also made him infamously famous in the industry. His motive to start PerezHilton.com was to mainly talk about celebrities and their personal life. He frequently appears on celebrity shows and other events, which give a major push to his blog.

A classic case of a hobby turned into a money-making job, PerezHilton.com generates around half a million dollars in monthly income through sponsored advertisements featured across the site, attracting over 6 million in monthly online visitors.

9. Univision Communications: Gizmodo

Another masterpiece created by Peter Rojas of Engadget fame, Gizmodo was actually launched before Engadget in 2002 as a blog focused on science and technology. It currently features articles on design, science fiction, technology and even political happenings.

Over a period of time, Gizmodo was launched in multiple languages by Gawker Media and VNU, including Dutch, French, German, Spanish, Portuguese and Italian. Gizmodo Brazil was launched in 2008 and another version was launched in 2011 to cover British news, as Gizmodo UK. In 2016, Univision Communications acquired Gawker Media and along with it, Gizmodo, later making it a flagship website under Gizmodo Media Group.

Gizmodo makes money by showing paid targeted advertisements along with sponsored articles. While it clocks in a monthly revenue of over $325,000, it sees a monthly average blog traffic of over 74 million! Over 35% of this traffic is through direct Google search, while around 13% is through referral sites.

10. Smashing Magazine

Founded in 2006 by Sven Lennartz and Vitaly Friedman, Smashing Magazine is an online hub of content for web developers and designers. It features a comprehensive resource center of information on graphic design, UI/UX and web development. The content is published in the form of articles as well as ebooks, which is one of the main sources of income for the blog.

Smashing Magazine launched the Smashing Library in 2012 that includes more than 50 ebooks and video tutorials on web designing, coding, design trends and many more related topics. The portal also conducts industry conferences annually in four cities – New York City, Barcelona, San Francisco and Freiburg (Germany). These conferences are sponsored by industry giants and are attended by the who's who of the domain, and host discussions on trends in web designing and development.

Smashing Magazine also works as a job portal for designers and developers, connecting the employers and prospective employees. In fact, in 2015, it was ranked as one of the best places for companies to find professional web designers by The Huffington Post.

Generating a monthly revenue of over $215,000, Smashing Magazine witnesses a monthly traffic load of over 4 million visitors on its website, smashingmagazine.com.

Looking at the top 10 highest paid bloggers, we can safely say that the competition is cut throat due to the abundance of content already out there. Most popular domains in which bloggers are earning handsomely are technology and marketing. That also means the fight to be at the top within these domains is intense and the editors and writers of these blogs have to always be on their toes to churn out unique and quality content.

Chapter Six
All The Best Monetization Strategies

To become the kind of blogger that makes more money in one month than your parents did in an entire year, it takes more than just quality content.

It takes building trust with your readers so they believe you and follow your advice when you recommend a new product or service to buy.

The old sales adage is nobody likes to be sold, but everyone likes to buy.

70% of the customers in one particular case study stated that they are more likely to buy something when they see content about a product or service shared by a friend.

Why?

Because there is a sense of trust there and you feel more inclined to try something you may not have otherwise because someone you believe in has vouched for the product. No list of successful bloggers is ever complete without Pat Flynn. He's a pioneer of sorts when it comes to this topic, especially because he is actually one of the first to ever begin posting a monthly income report to his blog.

Before we go any further, I need to tell you that his margins are extremely impressive. Pat himself says on his website that he did not get to where he is overnight. You need to keep this in mind when you begin the transition from "hobby" to "lucrative career path". You most likely will not wake up tomorrow having earned $10,000 in your sleep.

Pat is a proof, however, that hard work and determination do pay off. His website has consistently earned him over $100,000 per month since January of 2015.

To fully understand where these numbers come from, we should take a look at his April 2016 income report.

❖ **Strategy 1: $58,575/month through affiliation with BlueHost**

BlueHost is an inexpensive and easy domain and web hosting company. It is especially great for beginners, which makes it a potentially lucrative opportunity for more experienced bloggers to make some money. Their affiliate marketing program is one of the best, too. They offer $65 per sale to their affiliates!

Affiliate marketing is not a new idea. As a matter of fact, referrals just like this one was ranked 3rd in the top US marketing for the shopping industry, affecting 23.26% of sales in 2014 alone. People trust people, and if a figure in "authority" backs a product, that may be all it takes for a person to take the plunge and make a purchase.

In Pat's case, as he has already proven himself to be a trustworthy and successful blogger, his BlueHost affiliation has really taken off, earning him over $58,000 in April of 2016 alone.

The best part? It's all passive income.

After signing up for the affiliate program with BlueHost, Pat placed his BlueHost affiliate links strategically around his blog. He made a 4-minute YouTube video that teaches people how to install WordPress and set up a domain and hosting account. To date, the video has been viewed over 200,000 times. He has also included the link in various other how-to's and tutorial pages on his website.

In July of 2011, Pat even shared with his audience the list of places he included his affiliation links and how many referrals in one month alone he had received from each link.

❖ **Strategy 2: $12,675/month through podcast sponsorships**

Pat's SPI podcast, which came to fruition in July of 2010, started at a time when podcasts weren't all that popular. Sponsorships were all but unheard of for a number of reasons.

For starters, podcasts weren't a proven concept and lacked a loyal audience. Furthermore, it was expensive and difficult to set them up, which meant that they were a rarity in the blogging medium.

Fast forward six years, however, and podcasts are all the rage. One may even argue that they are now just beginning to reach the height of their popularity, which means that advertisers have a unique advantage to promote their products. This is where sponsorships come in. 67% of podcast listeners say they don't mind the occasional promotional message during their podcast.

Pat noticed this and took advantage. As of April 2016, his podcast sponsorships made up over $12,000 of his monthly income.

❖ Strategy 3: $12,405/month by licensing a custom

podcast player

Just when you start to think Pat Flynn can't possibly have enough hours in the day, he proves you wrong by building and licensing his own custom podcast player. If you are especially computer savvy, creating your own software can actually be a great way to make extra money.

People won't just pour their money into anything, though. First, you must find a problem and have your software solve that problem. That's exactly what Pat Flynn did with his Smart Podcast Player.

He noticed that his blog was directly receiving over 3 million podcast plays. He also noticed that the large number of plays were negatively impacting front-end experience for his audience. He saw a problem and set out to solve it.

After building a custom player for his podcast, Pat began to receive hundreds upon hundreds of requests from other podcast creators, all of whom wanted to use his product for their own podcasts.

The beta product launched in June of 2014 before being released to the public in January of 2015. Just shy of a year later, the product still manages to give Pat over $12,000 per month through licensing deals!

Abby Lawson of JustAGirlAndHerBlog makes over $36k per month

Abby Lawson just a girl and her blog for blog monetization strategies. With just about 3 years of blogging experience under her belt, Abby has managed to successfully monetize on her passion of DIY products and home decor. As with most bloggers, hers started as little more than a part-time hobby to get her ideas out there. She even shares her story of going from passion project blog to full time business in a popular post on her website, entitled "My Blogging Story".

Now, her blog is a wildly successful full time job for not only her, but her husband as well. In her About page, she explains just how "wrong" her website name, Just A Girl And Her Blog, is... Because her entire family works hard to keep the business running strong.

Taking a look at her income reports since February of 2014, it is astounding to see the gradual growth and how far Abby and her blog have come since conception. Now, with over $35,000 per month in profit, Abby is considered a top blogger in the business, and has proven that her business model works.

❖ Strategy 4: $10,668/month by selling e-books

Yes, Abby is a blogger. Yes, bloggers write. But even the high level of quality and content on Abby's blog can't compare to that of a full length book.

She has written 3 e-books, each of which offer a unique insight into various niches. The first deals with building a successful blog. The second deals with organizing your life through Evernote. The third is a "resource" that contains 35 printables to help organize your life.

Each individual e-book sells for between $10 and $20. However, Abby also very smartly includes "packages", so her loyal audience can get a deal in purchasing more than one item – Incentive to spend more, I say! Abby is living proof that you can indeed make a living from selling e-books.

The difference between a new blogger and someone like Abby is the loyal audience she has established. She was fortunate enough to receive a book deal because of her proven following. People will buy her book simply because her name is attached to it and they trust her.

❖ **Strategy 5: $5,070/month selling a PDF life planner on Amazon**

Not all products have to have an infinite shelf life. Abby managed to make some quick money over the 2015 holiday season by selling a PDF life planner. She announced the product in November of 2015 as a way to help her audience gain control of their lives and stay organized and productive throughout the new year.

With a relatively low price point (it was priced at just $10), the response to the product was overall positive. She made over $5,000 by selling this planner in the month of November, another $2,100 in December, and still continued to sell $2,240 of the product through January of 2016. Not bad, right?

You don't have to sell a life planner, either. Any product that will add some value to your customers' life will do. In a sense, people are buying into your brand – not necessarily the product.

John Lee Dumas, who managed to make the 6th most funded Kickstarter publishing campaign of all time when he launched a Kickstarter project to help launch "The Freedom Journal" – a resource to help his audience reach their goal in just 100 days.

The journal's "packs", which ranged in price from $35 to nearly $300, raised over $453,000 in Kickstarter funds in just 33 days.

There is a demand for these kinds of products, so why not get involved with them?

❖ Strategy 6: $175/45 minutes with one-on-one phone coaching

Just take a look at those margins and let it sink in. For one 45 minute phone conversation with Johnny, a person is shelling out $175.

That's just one of the packages that Johnny offers in his one-on-one phone coaching. He offers four separate ways for people to get in contact with him, so you can actually spend up to $800 on his services if you have the money. These may seem a bit steep in price, and I wouldn't necessarily blame you for wondering if anyone would shell out this kind of money for a phone call with you, but I want to take a look at the advantages of these phone conversations from a customer's point of view before we continue any further.

Mentoring is important for a lot of reasons. It can shorten the learning curve for a newbie, it can help you get some insight from a "professional" that you otherwise wouldn't have had, and it can help you if you have a problem that you otherwise wouldn't be able to solve.

Although these mentoring sessions aren't included in his most recent income reports, it is still worth noting that this could potentially be a great service to offer your audience.

You may not be able to charge the price that Johnny, an already established and trusted blogger, does, but that doesn't mean that you can't offer the service at all. Even charging a portion of Johnny's price (maybe starting out at $99 per hour) means you will probably get a few bites. From there, you can build your credibility, and even possibly gain some repeat customers.

❖ Strategy 7: $264/month by selling an e-book in Spanish

We've already discussed the importance of having an established following when it comes to selling e-books and getting a book deal. But once you have that deal, how can you monetize further? Johnny came up with quite an interesting idea when he decided to re-write and sell his book, 'Life Changes Quick', in Spanish.

He capitalized on the importance of gaining a lot of momentum very fast. Instead of letting his book fizzle, he repackaged and resold it in another language in order to gain more of an audience, and perhaps even connect with people he wouldn't have been able to otherwise.

Let's be honest: this is not his biggest money maker, nor is it enough to sustain his lifestyle. It is, however, an important lesson to note. If you are interested in writing a book and need some help, Tim Ferris compiled an extensive resource on how to write a bestseller that you should definitely take a look at.

❖ Strategy 8: $184/month from Udemy courses.

Information sells. Just like we saw with the power of the e-book, people will pay a premium to receive information from a trusted source.

No one out there right now does it quite as uniquely as

Udemy. What sets this online course website apart from the others on the market is its business model. It's something of an online course marketplace, if you will, which pools students and instructors alike under one platform.

After you make your course and put it on the site, all you have to do is sit back and wait for someone to bite. Every single time someone pays for your course, you receive 70% of the revenue forever.

There is no shelf life of these courses, and they can sit in the system for all of eternity, while you do nothing but collect the money that piles in from it.

❖ **Strategy 9: $4,659/month from dropshipping stores**

Dropshipping is what Johnny considers to be "semi-passive" income. Why, you ask? Because although the majority of his earnings happen while he is away from his computer and having absolutely nothing having to do with them, he does spend "a few hours a week" working on the store and handling customer service inquiries.

Johnny himself suggests that newbies do a bit of research before diving in. He even recommends this course (yes, he is an affiliate!) if you need some extra help. Additionally, Johnny wrote a beginner's article on the subject that you can read right here.

The coolest thing about dropshipping stores is just how valuable they become once you get profitable. How valuable, you ask? Try upwards of six figures.

❖ Strategy 10: $5,475/month by selling an online class

Yet again, we are faced with the fact that information sells. 50 Workdays – Zero to Blog, the self-guided class that Regina founded, is one of her biggest money makers.

Although she no longer posts income reports, it is safe to say that this class in particular has been a success for her — she relaunched it earlier this year under the name Epic Blog Crew.

The thought of starting your own online class and having a bunch of people learn from you can be pretty daunting. You probably don't have a teaching degree, and who's to say that you are the right person to learn from? Well, the people buying your class would beg to differ!

In order to sell a class that people want to buy, you must validate your worth. Be someone who they want to learn from, and people will pay to hear what you have to say. Here's the foolproof method: create a blog on a niche that you are knowledgeable and passionate about, write some unique, interesting, thought provoking material (no pressure, right?), garner some email subscribers, and build a loyal following.

It won't happen overnight, and it won't always be easy. It will, however, be satisfying when you finally manage to get that first 1,000 subscribers. After you have managed to gain a loyal following, all you have to do is look at the analytical side of it – what does your audience want to know?

To truly understand the answer to that question, you can look no further than your most viewed posts. Whatever posts have become the most popular on your blog should probably be the basis of your online course. It's a proven method that works and you already know that it has the potential to earn money, as people are searching for it.

❖ Strategy 11: $3,224/month by selling an editorial planner

Similar to what Abby did with her life planner, Regina went out and sold a physical editorial planner. The difference between the two products, however, is that Regina's planner is a year-round business venture.

At a price point of $18.50, and sold both on her website and on Amazon, the planner is wholly affordable to people who buy into her brand and products. It was largely successful on Amazon and boasted a 81% 5 star customer review.

Selling these kinds of items also helps you to build a brand outside of the internet — Blogging is great, but it is important to establish yourself in other mediums as well. Regina proves this by selling multiple products in the same wheelhouse. She offers a number of workbooks and guides, ranging from just $5 to $30 in price.

❖ Strategy 12: $237/month by selling products via Amazon Affiliate Program

I realize that $237 a month isn't an astounding amount of money and that no single person could sustain their lifestyle on that revenue. But Regina's monthly Amazon income is NOT representative of the majority.

The program pays up to 8.5% commission on all sales, which makes it especially valuable to niche bloggers who want to make some extra cash. How does it work, you ask? It's simple.

The most important thing to remember when you are selling products via Amazon Affiliates is that you should:

a) only promote products you truly believe in, and

b) never be pushy.

Always integrate your links into a how-to article of some kind and never, ever outwardly tell your readers to buy something so you can earn a little extra cash. If you are a DIY blogger and you are posting a how-to on mason jar candles, for example, you may want to include an Amazon Affiliates link to the specific glue gun tools you used throughout the process. That's it.

Trust that your audience will believe in your brand enough to make the purchase without you insulting their intelligence and blatantly shoving it down their throats.

Mistakes To Avoid

Sometimes, when I tell people that I blog for a living, they roll their eyes. "That's so easy," they say. "You get a paycheck for sitting on the internet all day and writing. A monkey could do your job!"

That's when I roll my eyes. See, people are quick to deem blogging as a no-brainer job. But when they actually sit down to write their first couple of posts, it hits them: This is way harder than I thought. Like any person starting a new job, they mess things up.

That's okay -- it happens to pretty much every new blogger. Luckily, it's pretty easy to avoid these roadblocks if you know they're coming.

1. Create blog posts that serve your larger company goals.

Mistake: You think of ideas that only interest you.

As much as you might read and re-read your blog posts after you publish them, you're not the only reader, or the intended reader.

When you start blogging, ideas will come to you at random times -- in the shower, on a run, while on the phone with your mom. While the ideas may come at random moments, the ideas themselves should never be random. Just because it's a good idea in general -- or something that interests you personally -- doesn't mean it's a good idea for your company.

Solution: Align your blog posts with company growth goals.

The reason you're blogging is to solve problems for your audience and, ultimately, to grow your business. So, all of your blog post ideas should help serve those growth goals. They should have natural tie-ins to issues in your industry and address specific questions and concerns your prospects have.

Need help figuring out what those goals are and how to address them? Chat with your manager about the larger company goals, and then schedule a meeting with someone on the sales team to hear what questions they get asked most often. After both meetings, you should know which goals you need to achieve and have some ideas on how to achieve them.

2. Write like you talk.

Mistake: Your writing is too stiff.

Writing a blog post is much different than writing a term paper. But when bloggers first start out, they usually only have experience with the latter. The problem? The style of writing from a term paper is not the style of writing people enjoy reading.

Let's be honest: Most of the people who see your post aren't going to read the whole thing. If you want to keep them interested, you have to compel them to keep reading by writing in a style that's effortless to read.

Solution: Try to write blogs that feel personable.

It's okay to be more conversational in your writing -- in fact, we encourage it. The more approachable your writing is, the more people will enjoy reading it. People want to feel like they're doing business with real people, not robots.

So loosen up your writing. Throw in contractions. Get rid of the jargon. Make a pun or two. That's how real people talk -- and that's what real people like to read.

3. Show your personality; don't tell it.

Mistake: You think people care about you as a writer.

It sounds harsh, but it's the truth: When people first start out blogging, they think that their audience will be inherently interested in their stories and their interests ... but that's not the case. It's no knock against them as a person -- it's just that when you're new, no one is interested in you and your experiences. People care way more about what you can teach them.

Solution: Infuse your personality without eclipsing the topic.

Even though people don't really care that it's you that's writing the post, you can infuse parts of your personality in your writing to make them feel more comfortable with you. How you do that is entirely up to you. Some people like to crack jokes, some like to make pop culture references, and others have a way with vivid descriptions.

To infuse personality into your own writing, try looking for ways to relate to your readers on the topic you're writing about -- then write in the first person as if you're hanging out with them and chatting about it. Make your tone personal, approachable, and engaging, just like you would in a face-to-face conversation.

4. Make your point again and again.

Mistake: You digress.

Although you are encouraged to let your own personality shine through in your writing, don't abuse the privilege. It's one thing to be yourself in the topic you're covering, but it's another thing to bring up too many personal experiences that bury the point you're trying to make.

Don't digress into these personal anecdotes and analogies too much -- your readers aren't sitting in front of you, which means you can't guarantee that you have their undivided attention. They can (and will) bounce from your article if they lose patience.

Solution: Repeatedly assert your argument.

To prevent your writing from losing its audience, restate your point in every section of the article. The best blog posts commit to an overarching message and then deliver it gradually, expressing it multiple times in small ways from beginning to end.

If you're writing about how much water a potted plant needs, for example, don't spend three paragraphs telling a story of how you came home to a dead fern after returning from a two-week vacation. This story offers real evidence of your point, but what is your point? Certain plants can't go without water for more than 14 days. That's one possible point, and it should be stated upfront.

5. Start with a very specific working title.

Mistake: Your topics are too broad.

When people start blogging, they generally want to write on really big topics like:

- ✓ "How to Do Social Media Marketing"
- ✓ "Business Best Practices"
- ✓ "How to Make Money on the Internet"

Topics like these are far too broad. Because there are so many details and nuances in these topics, it's really hard to do a good job answering them. Plus, more specific topics tend to attract smaller, more targeted audiences, which tend to be higher quality and more likely to convert into leads and customers.

So, to get the most short-term and long-term benefits of blogging, you'll need to get way more specific.

Solution: Begin with a clear, concise idea.

Nailing really specific blog topics is crucial to knocking

your first few posts out of the park. Let us help you brainstorm with our Blog Ideas Generator. This tool allows you to enter basic terms you want to cover, and then produces five sample blog titles that work for business blogs.

Keep in mind that a working title isn't final -- it's just a concrete angle you can use to keep your writing on track. Once you nail this stage of the ideation process, it's much easier to write your blog posts.

6. Use a specific post type, create an outline, and use headers.

Mistake: Your writing is a brain dump.

Sometimes when I get a great idea I'm excited about, it's really tempting to just sit down and let it flow out of me. But what I get is usually a sub-par blog post.

Why? The stream-of-consciousness style of writing isn't really a good style for blog posts. Most people are going to scan your blog posts, not read them, so it needs to be organized really well for that to happen.

Solution: Structure your blog with a template, outline, and section headers.

The first thing you should do is choose what type of blog post you're going to write. Is it a how-to post? A list-based post? A curated collection post? A SlideShare presentation?

Once you have a template down, it'll be easier to write your outline.

Writing an outline makes a big difference. If you put in the time up front to organize your thoughts and create a logical flow in your post, the rest becomes easy -- you're basically just filling in the blanks.

To write a blog post outline, first come up with a list of the top takeaways you want your readers to get from your post. Then, break up those takeaways into larger section headers. When you put in a section header every few paragraphs, your blog post becomes easier and more enjoyable to read. (And plus, header text with keywords is good for SEO.) When you finally get to writing, all you'll have to do is fill in those sections.

7. Use data and research to back up the claims you make in your posts.

Mistake: You don't use data as evidence.

Let's say I'm writing a blog post about why businesses should consider using Instagram for marketing. When I'm making that argument, which is more convincing?

- ✓ "It seems like more people are using Instagram nowadays."

- ✓ "Instagram's user base is growing far faster than social network usage in general in the U.S. Instagram will grow 15.1% this year, compared to just 3.1% growth for the social network sector as a whole."

The second, of course. Arguments and claims are much more compelling when rooted in data and research. As marketers, we don't just have to convince people to be on our side about an issue -- we need to convince them to take action. Data-driven content catches people's attention in a way that fluffy arguments do not.

Solution: Use data to support your arguments.

In any good story, you'll offer a main argument, establish proof, and then end with a takeaway for the audience. You can use data in blog posts to introduce your main argument and show why it's relevant to your readers, or as proof of it throughout the body of the post.

Some great places to find compelling data include:

- ✓ HubSpot Research
- ✓ Pew Research Center
- ✓ MarketingSherpa
- ✓ HubSpot's State of Inbound report

8. When drawing from others' ideas, cite them.

Mistake: Your content borders on plagiarism.

Plagiarism didn't work in school, and it certainly doesn't work on your company's blog. But for some reason, many beginner bloggers think they can get away with the old copy-and-paste technique.

You can't. Editors and readers can usually tell when something's been copied from somewhere else. Your voice suddenly doesn't sound like you, or maybe there are a few words in there that are incorrectly used. It just sounds ... off.

Plus, if you get caught stealing other people's content, you could get your site penalized by Google -- which could be a big blow to your company blog's organic growth.

Solution: Give credit where credit is due.

Instead, take a few minutes to understand how to cite other people's content in your blog posts. It's not super complicated, but it's an essential thing to learn when you're first starting out.

9. Take 30 minutes to edit your post.

Mistake: You think you're done once the writing's done.

Most people make the mistake of not editing their writing. It sounded so fluid in their head when they were writing that it must be great to read ... right?

Nope -- it still needs editing. And maybe a lot of it.

Solution: You'll never regret time spent proofreading.

Everyone needs to edit their writing -- even the most experienced writers. Most times, our first drafts aren't all that great. So take the time you need to shape up your post. Fix typos, run-on sentences, and accidental its/it's mistakes. Make sure your story flows just as well as it did in your outline.

To help you remember all the little things to check before publishing, check out our checklist for editing and proofreading a blog post.

10. At a certain point, just publish it.

Mistake: You try to make every post perfect.

I hate to break it to you, but your blog post is never going to be perfect. Ever.

There will always be more things you can do to make your posts better. More images. Better phrasing. Wittier jokes. The best writers I know, know when to stop obsessing and just hit "publish".

Solution: Better to publish and update than postpone for perfection.

There's a point at which there are diminishing returns for getting closer to "perfect" -- and you're really never going to reach "perfect" anyway. So while you don't want to publish a post filled with factual inaccuracies and grammatical errors, it's not the end of the world if a typo slips through. It most likely won't affect how many views and leads it brings in.

Plus, if you (or your readers) find the mistake, all you have to do is update the post. No biggie. So give yourself a break once in a while -- perfect is the enemy of done.

11. Blog consistently with the help of an editorial calendar.

Mistake: You don't blog consistently.

By now, you've probably heard that the more often you blog, the more traffic you'll get to your website -- and the more subscribers and leads you'll generate from your posts. But as important as volume is, it's actually more important that you're blogging consistently when you're just getting started. If you publish five posts in one week and then only one or two in the next few weeks, it'll be hard to form a consistent habit. And inconsistency could really confuse your subscribers.

Instead, it's the companies that make a commitment to regularly publishing quality content to their blogs that tend to reap the biggest rewards in terms of website traffic and leads -- and those results continue to pay out over time.

To help establish consistency, you'll need a more concrete planning strategy.

Solution: Schedule and publish blogs consistently.

Use it to get into the habit of planning your blog post topics ahead of time, publishing consistently, and even scheduling posts in advance if you're finding yourself having a particularly productive week.

12. Focus on the long-term benefits of organic traffic.

Mistake: You concentrate your analytics on immediate traffic.

Both beginner bloggers and advanced bloggers are guilty of this blogging mistake. If you concentrate your analysis on immediate traffic (traffic from email subscribers, RSS feeds, and social shares), then it's going to be hard to prove the enduring value of your blog. After all, the half-life for those sources is very brief -- usually a day or two.

When marketers who are just starting their business blogs see that their blog posts aren't generating any new traffic after a few days, many of them get frustrated. They think their blog is failing, and they end up abandoning it prematurely.

Solution: The ROI of your blog is the aggregation of organic traffic over time.

Instead of focusing on the sudden decay of short-term traffic, focus instead on the cumulative potential of organic traffic. Over time, given enough time, the traffic from day three and beyond of a single blog post will eclipse that big spike on days one and two thanks to being found on search engine results pages through organic search. You just have to give it a while.

To help drive this long-term traffic, make sure you're writing blog posts that have durable relevance on a consistent basis. These posts are called "evergreen" blog posts: They're relevant year after year with little or no upkeep, valuable, and high quality.

Over time, as you write more evergreen content and build search authority, those posts will end up being responsible for a large percentage of your blog traffic. It all starts with a slight shift in perspective from daily traffic to cumulative traffic so you can reframe the way you view your blog and its ROI entirely.

13. Add a subscription CTA to your blog and set up an email newsletter.

Mistake: You aren't growing subscribers.

Once you start blogging, it's easy to forget that blogging isn't just about getting new visitors to your blog. One of the biggest benefits of blogging is that it helps you steadily grow an email list of subscribers you can share your new content with. Each time you publish a new blog post, your subscribers will give you that initial surge of traffic -- which, in turn, will propel those posts' long-term success.

The key to getting significant business results (traffic, leads, and eventually customers) starts with growing subscribers.

Solution: How to set up a subscription CTA and email newsletter:

First, use your email marketing tool to set up a welcome email for new subscribers, as well as a regular email that pulls in your most recent blog posts. (HubSpot customers: You can use HubSpot's email tool to easily set up these regular email sends, as well as set up a welcome email for new subscribers.)

Next, add subscription CTAs to your blog (and elsewhere, like the footer of your website) to make it easy for people to opt in. These CTAs should be simple, one-field email opt-in forms near the top of your blog, above the fold.

Conclusion

To summarize it all, you can monetize your blog with five different methods, namely:

- ✓ Affiliate marketing
- ✓ Displaying Ads
- ✓ Selling services and products
- ✓ Sponsored posts
- ✓ Paid Reviews

In this book, you have learned that monetizing your blog goes beyond advertisements. Monetizing blog with just advertisements is like squandering the potential of your blog.

Finally, monetizing your blog will only get better in the long run. Therefore, you should not rush into anything and just take it one step at a time.

That is all you need to know to start monetizing your blog!

www.ingramcontent.com/pod-product-compliance
Lightning Source LLC
LaVergne TN
LVHW022323060326
832902LV00020B/3644